"Our one major goal is to create satisfied customers. Hence, all systems, objectives, training, and measurements are designed to improve customer satisfaction."

> — John A. Young,
> *President and CEO,*
> *Hewlett-Packard*

"Our objective is to give more and better service than our customers expect. This is more a matter of re-commitment to service excellence."

> — Joe Malone,
> *President,*
> *Prudential Life Insurance Company*

"One half of our business comes from repeat customers and one half from new customers, which we consider to be a healthy mix. If all business comes from new customers, you need to wonder what you're doing wrong."

> — Paul Newton,
> *President and CEO,*
> *Relational Technology*

"Customer satisfaction starts with the chief executive officer as a role model — talking, listening, responding, respecting, creating, and living the environment and having an open door to all employees at all times."

> — Steve Watson,
> *Chairman and CEO,*
> *Dayton-Hudson Department Stores*

Keep the Customer!

ROBERT L. DESATNICK

Keep the Customer!

*Making
Customer Service
Your Competitive Edge*

HOUGHTON MIFFLIN COMPANY

BOSTON

Copyright © 1987 by Jossey-Bass, Inc., Publishers
Preface copyright © 1990 by Robert L. Desatnick

All Rights Reserved

For information about permission to reproduce selections from this
book, write to Permissions, Jossey-Bass, Inc., Publishers, 350 Sansome,
San Francisco, CA 94104 & Jossey-Bass Limited, 28 Banner Street,
London EC1Y 8QE.

Library of Congress Cataloging-in-Publication Data

Desatnick, Robert L.
[Managing to keep the customer]
Keep the customer! : making customer service your competitive
edge / Robert L. Desatnick.
p.   cm.
"Originally published in slightly different form with the title:
Managing to keep the customer" — T.p. verso.
Includes bibliographical references.
ISBN 0-395-53809-2
1. Customer service.   2. Customer relations.   I. Title.
HF5415.5.D47   1990   89-49204
658.8'12 — dc20   CIP

Printed in the United States of America

BTA 10 9 8 7 6 5 4 3 2 1

Houghton Mifflin Paperback 1990

To my wife, Margo L. Bennett,
my dearest friend and colleague,
who gave so generously of her time
during my periods of absence in
putting this manuscript together

CONTENTS

PREFACE

Keep the Customer! is the key to surviving and prospering in today's highly competitive service marketplace.

We are in the midst of a service revolution. If anything, it will continue to intensify in the 1990s. To stay ahead and to become winners, businesses will need to distinguish themselves primarily with superior service. Excellent customer service will create and sustain the perceptible difference in this new competitive environment.

Despite a high mortality rate among new business ventures, most of the nation's economic growth has come from companies with fewer than 150 employees. The U.S. economy has produced 31 million new jobs since 1972. It will add another 21 million by the end of the century. As Louis Richman pointed out in an article in *Fortune* magazine, most of this growth will come from small, fast-growing companies. Furthermore, the U.S. Labor Department predicts that nine out of ten new jobs to be created over the next ten years will be in the service sector of our economy.

The evidence is overwhelming in terms of what it will take to come out on top in this atmosphere. Whether you have two, twenty, two hundred, or two hundred thousand employees, service throughout the organization is the new standard by which customers, suppliers, employees, and competitors are measuring organizational performance. Whether your organization is involved in manufacturing, distribution, sales, service, or other enterprises, the quality of service will provide that necessary competitive advantage to propel you to the top. Whether you are public or private, profit or not-for-profit, religious, social, or fraternal, managing service performance is critical to your economic well-being.

Peter Drucker, in his book *Managing in Turbulent Times*, tells us that the survivors are going to distinguish themselves in one of two ways: either through clear product superiority or through clear service superiority. Airline passengers automatically assume that the engines will work. Hospital patients assume that their respirators will work. The fact is that organizations are becoming increasingly dependent on distinguishing themselves on the basis of clear service superiority versus product superiority.

Customers' perceptions of your organization are reality; their feelings are facts. We're all in the service business; we're all in the business of service. This book shows you that good customer service depends on the employees in your organization and how they are managed. Employees, after all, have the most direct contact with customers. Hiring, training, and maintaining an effective work force are a manager's best means of keeping the customer happy. Customer satisfaction is defined as the degree of happiness a customer experiences with your product or service. It also reflects the quality of the interrelationships and interactions of all employees in every part of the organization.

Research for this book is based on studies of service role model organizations in more than 500 companies (small, medium, and large) in a variety of businesses and industries —

manufacturing as well as service. It encompasses approximately 250,000 employees over a period of seven years. It reveals successes, failures, and transformations. It indicates what to do right and what to avoid. It enables you to create or reinforce your organization to please customers both internally and externally.

Keep the Customer! explains the most successful management practices and policies of these service role model organizations. It is written for any organization that wishes to create an awareness of service superiority — to make a perceptible difference in its customers' minds with respect to its competitors. This is a hands-on book of tools, techniques, and methodologies aimed at management.

ROBERT L. DESATNICK
Chicago, Illinois
January 1990

Keep the Customer!

1

CUSTOMER SERVICE

❏ *The Real Competitive Edge*

Future historians may well describe the 1990s as the era of customer sovereignty. Perhaps "customer rebellion" is more accurate. Customers are rightfully insisting on getting what they paid for, whether it is a clean glass, an impeccable hotel room, a decent meal in the hospital, an on-time delivery, or courteous treatment at the point of purchase.

The business organizations that will succeed are those that recognize today's customer revolution and are fully prepared to meet the challenge at the highest standards of service. For any business or institution — public or private, for-profit or not-for-profit, service-oriented or product-oriented — now is the time to seize the competitive advantage.

It is time for every business to examine and reassess how well it manages its relationships with two key groups: internal customers (employees) and external customers (those who purchase its products or services). Both are essential; the two are inseparable. Any business that fails to take this preventive initiative, *before* market share, sales, or profits decline, may well find itself unable to reverse the downward trend.

It matters not whether a company is large, medium-size, or small. Trying to compete solely on the basis of product or price is insufficient. For one thing, product differentiation is becoming increasingly difficult; look at the airlines, hotels, fast foods, hospitals, banks, auto rentals, and on and on. How can they create a perceptible difference that sets them ahead of the pack? It usually is not product superiority. The key is service — attention to the customer. Service is the new standard by which customers are measuring an organization's performance. It is not *a* competitive edge, it is *the* competitive edge.

❑ Service Encounters of the Worst Kind

Imagine a typical day on a business trip and follow through the sequence of events.

What You Experience	*What Happens Afterward*
Your radio alarm fails.	"Sir, we only sell it; read your warranty."
You get a limo to take you to the airport.	The trunk is full of water and greasy tools. You soak your suit and garment bag.
You try to check in to claim your flight seat.	"Sorry, sir, this line is closed, move on."
You pick up your rental car.	"We're all out of compacts. Too bad, the car rattles."
You check into your hotel with a guaranteed reservation.	"Sorry, sir, you're not registered; we're full."

Breakfast is a half-hour late.

"Sorry, sir, it went to the wrong room."

At the office the photocopying machine is down.

It will take a few days to get it fixed.

The telephone is making funny noises.

"We'll have to schedule a repairman; can't say for sure when he'll be out."

Your answering service abruptly says, "Beep-beep, hold on."

You get cut off from a long distance call.

You ordered a hot sandwich for lunch.

The sandwich is cold and greasy.

You check out of the hotel — or try to.

Your bill is wrong; the breakfast charge was not added.

You finally pick up your baggage.

It is torn and broken.

❑ The Danger of Growth

A big part of the problem is corporate America's love affair with marketing. It is hard to pick up a newspaper or magazine these days without being deluged with information on marketing. There are many articles on such items as mature brand strategy, marketing innovation, advertising, product improvement, and product differentiation. But what about service to the existing customers?

Aggressive sales and marketing can get too far ahead of an organization's ability to provide required services on time. The mistake many service companies make when times are good is that they get so caught up in adding new customers and new services that they lose touch with the existing customer base. In their eagerness to grow, they take on more new accounts than they can service properly. Anxious to capture more market share, they neglect their old accounts and eventually lose part of that business to competition.

What is the net effect? A great deal of research on customer service has produced the fact that it is *five times* more expensive to get a new customer than to keep an old one. Putting it another way, the cost of losing a repeat customer is approximately five times the value of that annual account.

Organizations will spend literally hundreds of millions of dollars to attract new customers while their old customers slip out the back door, never to return again. What drives people away is rude, discourteous, inept, incompetent service. It may simply be a matter of apathy or inattention.

Now, it would seem logical that if an organization is willing to spend $100 million or more annually on advertising and sales promotion, it should be willing to spend just about $20 million to keep its present customers. In fact, outstanding service and its ensuing word of mouth will not only keep present customers but attract new ones as well.

If service is as important as chief executive officers claim it is, why is there not a vice president of customer service, on the same level as the vice presidents of sales and marketing?

❑ The High Cost of an Unhappy Customer

In today's fiercely competitive market, no business can long survive without satisfied customers. Let's look at some significant findings from a study conducted for the White House office of Consumer Affairs by TARP, a Washington, D.C., consultant:

- 96 percent of unhappy customers never complain about rude or discourteous treatment, *but*
- 90 percent or more who are dissatisfied with the service they receive will not buy again or come back. *Worse still,*
- each of those unhappy customers will tell his or her story to at least nine other people, *and*
- 13 percent of those unhappy former customers will tell their stories to more than twenty people.

The book *Service America* also credits TARP research in discussing the following price tags on customer loyalty. For instance, the automobile industry believes that a loyal customer represents a lifetime average revenue of $140,000. So why have a fight over a $20 repair bill or a $10 replacement part? In banking it is estimated that the average customer represents at least $80 a year in profit. In appliance manufacturing, brand loyalty is worth $2,800 over a twenty-year period. Your local supermarket counts on you for $4,400 within a given year. So why quibble about some little something that the customer thinks is not right? People who believe in service superiority make things right; they want their customers to come back.

❏ Doing It Right

Some companies already understand this, and have incorporated a full commitment to service superiority. Why do you suppose that Procter & Gamble has a toll-free number for customers' questions? Similarly, Neiman-Marcus has a "no questions asked" refund policy, some management consultants offer a money-back guarantee if customers are not satisfied, Holiday Inn proclaims, "If it's not right, it's on us," and Marriott Hotels give "I'm sorry" gift certificates if something goes wrong. McDonald's gives a refund or another hot sandwich to a dissatisfied customer, and IBM sends in an army of repair technicians to take care of its computers. Frito-Lay sends a truck out in a blizzard to deliver a case of potato chips, Rolls-Royce does not charge for a service call anywhere in the world if its cars fail to proceed, and Johnson & Johnson voluntarily accepted great financial loss on the recall of Tylenol. Levi Strauss treats its employees with respect, and Herman Miller allows its employees to negotiate standards for customer service. Motorola has a participative management policy, Dayton Hudson holds free public seminars on such topics as the changing role of women and the problems of the aged, and Weyco employees put their names on products they make.

Why? Because these companies all know that their major strategic weapon is added value to the customer through superior service. They are willing to admit an error, and they immediately take steps to correct it. They clearly recognize that customer relations mirror employee relations. They are all open to change; in fact they have institutionalized the process of change to avoid stagnation.

But what about organizations that do not yet have this cultural value of service? Can they manage to become customer-oriented? To redefine their key values in terms of the customer? And then to get all their executives, managers, supervisors, and employees fully committed to achieving those values? Can they profit from the successes of those at the top while avoiding the mistakes of those who did not survive?

The central thesis of this book is that they can. We are privileged to be living in an information age, when shared knowledge and experiences are readily available. Thus those in customer-oriented organizations have immediate access to the successes and failures of those who came — and went — before them.

❑ Doing It Wrong

Most organizations *say* they are close to the customer, but frankly, few are. This is witnessed over and over again with battles that are won and lost at the simplest level of customer contact — the point of purchase, which frequently is staffed by minimum-wage employees. If we could do a complete post-mortem on all the businesses that failed, I am convinced we would find that one of the most prevalent causes of failure was inadequate or discourteous service.

And just talking about service is not enough. How often have you seen situations like this?

The Promise	*The Delivery*
The warranty with teeth.	You will have to send it to the manufacturer, and it will take six to twelve weeks.
How well did we do?	That's not what you ordered? Are you sure?
The no-excuses guarantee.	We have no one registered by that name.
Satisfaction or your money back.	No sales slip, no return.
We really try harder.	Gift wrapping is in the basement, and it's extra.
We pride ourselves on the highest standards of customer service.	We don't have your reservation, and we can't give you a room without one.
We stand behind our products.	We only sell it, we don't service it.
No one delivers faster than we do.	Sorry, we lost your package.

Why does the delivery so often fail to fulfill the promise? Many companies, large and small, tend to forget. Too often they relegate the customer service function way down in the lower levels of the organization. Then they proceed to staff it with entry-level and unskilled people.

❏ The Success Formula

By way of contrast, the essence of McDonald's success was — and is — its focus on the customer. Its corporate values were, and still are, quality, service, cleanliness, and value. After more than thirty years, this has not changed. McDonald's found the success formula.

It is important to recognize that Kentucky Fried Chicken and White Castle were on the scene long before McDonald's, but they were surpassed. Why? Because McDonald's fully understands that superiority in customer service is really superiority in "people" practices.

We have long known about the direct impact of employee relations on productivity and participative management. But we are just beginning to recognize the magnitude of that impact on market share, sales, costs, profits, and customer relations. There is in fact no magic success formula as such. But there is this: if a company's own house is not in order, it is not possible to achieve customer service superiority.

❏ When Business Is Good, Make It Better

The rapid pace of the times in which we live is accompanied by constant change as a way of life. This virtually man-

dates that we do things differently from those who pre-
ceded us. In *Managing in Turbulent Times,* Peter Drucker
strongly suggests the need to "slough off yesterday." The time
to change and reassess, to question every aspect of our operations, is not, he says, when we are in trouble but while
we are successful. If a company waits until it is marginal,
it goes down proportionately more when the economy goes
down and comes up disproportionately less when the economy recovers. Once marginality sets in, it is almost impossible to recover market share and reverse the downward
trend.

Drucker notes that is is particularly important to reassess
management strategies and tactics after a long period of relative calm and predictability. Could he possibly be referring
to banks, hospitals, airlines, retailers, and insurance companies, for example? In these turbulent times, every service,
both internal and external, every process, and every activity
needs to be put on trial every few years. As a strategy he
suggests that all institutions — public and private, profit and
not-for-profit — examine how their customers define "value."
How is each institution perceived in relation to its competition?

□ Service Superstars Are Role Models

There are a number of organizations that appear to have
created service success and then proceeded to set new standards of superiority.

Today there are more than 15,000 McDonald's restaurants
in fifty countries. Each afternoon, all over the world, millions
of customers are greeted cheerfully and sincerely, as if they
were personal friends of the employees. And remember,

these are minimum wage employees, ranging in age from sixteen to seventy. Most of them are part-time, with no benefits and no tips. How does McDonald's do it?

McDonald's success story is partially the result of spending hundreds of millions of dollars in advertising and sales promotion each year. However, the main reason is meticulous attention to detail. It is much more an operations-oriented than a market-oriented company. This is not apparent to the consuming public. They only see the results, the cheerful smile.

By way of an overall summary, McDonald's commitment to service and to good human resource management begins at the corporate level and promotes these same philosophies in all the regions, districts, and offices, and every facility and every restaurant. The organization's customer-focused values are reinforced by its policies toward its own people.

- Strong customer-focused corporate values: quality, service, cleanliness, and value
- Team environment encouraging interdependence
- Emphasis on employee participation with rapid management response
- Exposure of all levels to upper management
- Management panels and audiovisuals
- Discussions by supervisor in charge
- Managers seen as coaches and counselors, not judges, juries, or critics
- Monthly supervisory meeting with department head to discuss people plans
- Vice president of individuality to keep company small and link management and employees
- Public recognition and rewards for achievement, such as president's award banquet, special attention to service

awards, anniversaries and promotions, officer's discretionary bonus, and healthy internal competition
- Job security through achievement
- Pay for performance
- Promotion from within
- Rapid promotion with frequent salary review
- Performance appraisals, reviews, and feedback to improve performance, pay, and advancement, and to help all employees see how well they are doing
- Appeal process: ombudsman
- Exit interviews for all who leave
- Philosophy of openness
- Open personnel records
- One cafeteria for all employees; no executive dining room
- Family atmosphere, clean and hygienic
- Continuous employee attitude surveys
- Communications replete: house organs, payroll stuffers, newsletters
- Educational assistance
- Select scholarships for children of outstanding employees
- Annual physical for employee and spouse
- Sabbatical vacations of eight weeks after ten years
- Paid employee referral program

Until recently, McDonald's did not share what goes on in its offices in Oak Brook, Illinois, or at Hamburger University, or in its restaurants. But a breakthrough was made when McDonald's joined in a survey sponsored by Citicorp. The seventeen participants were selected by Citicorp on the basis of their perceived service superiority and their management practices of special interest. Ninety managers were interviewed. The companies in the survey, the superstars in the world of service, included American and United airlines, RCA and Whirlpool, Avis, Hertz, and National car rentals, Citicorp, Walt Disney, McDonald's, Westin hotels, IBM, Hartford and John Hancock insurance companies, Sears, Speigel's, and Commonwealth Edison.

Just what did these service superstars have in common that made them so exceptional? What management policies and values produced the highest standards of service quality, timeliness, and delivery? And do those same values still hold true today? That is what this book is all about. It tells not only what these role models did, but how they managed to do it. It shares their management strategies and operational tactics.

Specifically, it is possible to distill ten characteristics that these companies share. These characteristics will be discussed in considerable detail in the chapters that follow, so for now we will simply list them. Each of the superstars

1. recognized the fact that employee relations mirror customer relations. If they were to be superior in customer service, they knew they had to be superior in their relationships with their employees.
2. created an awareness of the importance of customer service in the minds of their employees. Taught the need for satisfied customers from an employee's perspective: the customer is the ultimate paymaster.
3. developed and implemented support systems needed to teach and reinforce the expected behaviors.
4. recognized that everything that happens in an organization has an impact on customer service. Established interconnecting support systems throughout their organizations.
5. defined and implemented precise and demanding performance standards, coupled with high performance expectations, to translate concepts to behavior.
6. trained managers, supervisors, and employees to rein-

force and maintain those desired behaviors once they had been established.

7. defined carefully the roles of managers and supervisors in promoting continuous service superiority.

8. provided tangible and intangible recognition and rewards for exemplary behavior. Made employees feel important and appreciated.

9. used quantitative measures to monitor the effectiveness of service and of personnel policies, practices, programs, and procedures.

10. built in strong, continuing reinforcement to sustain customer-oriented value systems and management practices.

In particular, these superstar companies developed certain human resource policies and practices that produced an outstanding commitment to service excellence.

To build accountability among all employees, so that they believe "each of us is the company," interviewed companies formally indoctrinate employees about accountability, reward actions beyond the call of duty, commend employees for formal customer compliments, and back up their employees' decisions made when interacting with customers. They also route customer feedback to appropriate employees and route errors and problems back to the specific employees causing them. They frequently appraise individual performance, and they practice justified firing in the context of a responsible grievance system. As a result of these actions, the companies' employees understand the scope of their personal responsibility and the importance of every service interaction and take pride in their jobs and their professionalism.

To create a service team, interviewed companies commemorate employees joining the team with special events and hold informative and motivational team assemblies. They broadly define and satisfy employees' need to know, inform employees how their jobs fit into the entire organization, and quickly disseminate information. They also frequently assess work group performance with employees. As a result of these actions, the companies minimize buck passing, strengthen their capacity to respond to change, and develop group trust.

To build open communications, companies use employee attitude surveys, promote suggestion programs, require frequent staff meetings within work groups, train employees in transactional analysis, and share customer reactions with the entire organization. As a result of these actions, they open multiple communication channels, strengthen employees' abilities to communicate effectively, and use these channels to identify problems and expedite their resolution.

Finally, to make major investments in human capital, the companies professionalize service personnel in a multiphase process, promote employees from within the organization, use a structured, in-house program for management training, and recognize and reward outstanding service to customers with meaningful incentive systems. As a result of these actions, the companies develop employees with the necessary service skills and stimulate continued allegiance to company goals and standards.

❑ Business Teaching Business

Service superiority begins with a restless dissatisfaction with the status quo. It starts at the top with those who say, "We can and will do better." From then on it is a matter of designing the corporate value system and building these values into every aspect of the employment contract.

It literally begins with hiring the right people, with an initial selection system through a patterned interview to select those individuals who share management's values. And it never stops.

The question that this book addresses is, Can any organization achieve comparable results? The answer is yes! If senior management is committed to establishing and reinforcing new standards of service superiority in all that is done, the dream can become a reality. Trial and error is no longer necessary, because through a process of compressing the collective experience, business organizations are able to distill and synthesize those ingredients that have worked well in building customer-oriented management systems for other companies.

There is an added plus for those organizations that strive to be the best at everything they do. In my observation, they seem inevitably to lead their industries in productivity, service superiority, cost effectiveness, employee morale, and loyalty. Not to mention profits.

CUSTOMER RELATIONS MIRROR EMPLOYEE RELATIONS

❑ *Developing Effective Human Resource Practices*

The single greatest source of profit growth in the 1990s will come from better management of human resources. Organizations that fail to recognize this and to prepare properly may well fall behind in the profit race, perhaps even disappear. This is not just my prophecy, but the expert opinion of the Research Institute. My own private research suggests that 80 percent of the opportunity for productivity and profitability improvement lies in effective management of the work force. A work force committed to excellence in customer service — internally and externally — will provide most of that opportunity.

Managing an organization's human resources equates with managing its customer services. To put it another way, employee relations equals customer relations. The two are inseparable.

Personnel and human resource executives have for some time been aware of the relationship between motivated employees and productivity. Only recently, however, have they been able to quantify this impact. Now they have begun to position themselves as part of the senior management team, and in the process they are addressing a broader range of business needs — customer service and customer satisfaction, cost containment, and management of the work force.

David E. Bowen of the University of Southern California's Department of Management and Organization examined the notion that taking care of human relations equates with taking care of the business. His sample population consisted of two groups of branch banks; one group had twenty-three and the other twenty-eight. Here is what he found:

- There is a strong correlation between customer and employee views of service quality and the internal climate for service.
- When employees view favorably an organization's human resource policies, customers view favorably the quality of service they receive.
- A positive work climate directly affects customer service for the better.
- Human resources is an excellent vehicle for satisfying both employee and customer needs.

Many organizations are just now becoming aware of the impact employee relations has on customer service. This chapter addresses that impact and provides ideas on how to ensure that the impact is positive.

❑ Step One: Put Your Own House in Order

To enjoy the highest standards of service superiority, organizations must have motivated employees. To have motivated employees, they must have motivated supervisors and managers. To have motivated supervisors and managers, organizations must first put their own internal houses in order. To complete the loop, putting one's own house in order requires exceptionally cordial relationships between management and labor. This is the key. If it is ignored — which all too often it is — relationships break down and a disastrous strike may occur, wreaking havoc on customer service. When relationships of openness and trust degenerate, the customer suffers as much as management and labor — maybe more.

❑ What Does It Take?

If we accept the premise that superiority in customer service starts with superior employee relations, how do we put that into practice? What does it take to cultivate and maintain outstanding employee relations?

For openers, there is relatively little we do know about employee needs, wants, and expectations. For many years we have correctly identified the relationship between levels of productivity and satisfaction of those needs. Now it is time to relate these employee needs to the effect on the customer, the ultimate paymaster.

To have motivated employees who will satisfy motivated customers and bring in new business and repeat business, employers must successfully address the major areas of employees' concerns. Traditionally, these concerns have been identified as good bosses, communications, working conditions, compensation, policy and administration, job security, achievement, recognition for achievement, involvement, participation, and advancement. Unfortunately, relatively few companies have paid more than just lip service to these basics, and as a consequence their employees have responded with poor service to the customer.

Let's look at these concerns individually, particularly their relationship to customer service.

Good Bosses

For a leading producer of household consumer goods, I have designed and conducted management skills training sessions for hourly and exempt nonsupervisory employees. For the most part these were high-potential people who were being prepared to assume broader responsibilities, including supervision. Over a period of two and a half years each group was asked to define a good boss. Here is a composite they came up with:

- Someone who cares about me and my progress.
- Someone I can trust to teach and develop me.
- Someone who supports me.
- Someone who corrects me when I need it.
- Someone who shows me how to do a better job.
- Someone who recognizes and rewards my achievement.
- Someone who keeps me informed about what's going on.
- Someone who consults with me on decisions affecting my job.
- Someone who trusts me by delegating real responsibility.

To further test what employees want and expect from a good boss, I conducted twenty-nine focus groups of 150 people each, as part of an assignment to design a selection system and management skills training program. From one group of employees in a service business, more than half the participants said, in effect, "Here is what I consider a good boss."

Considerate	Treats me with respect
Fair	Gives me recognition

Honest	Appreciates me
Just	Uses tact and diplomacy
Caring	Has stature in the organization
Impartial	Maintains high standards of discipline
Communicative	and work
Interested	Sets a good example
Calm	Empathizes
Friendly	Does not scream or yell
Available	Delegates
Consistent	Is a problem solver
Trusting	Is a good listener

Communications

There are two major aspects of the internal communication processes that exert a tremendous influence on customer service: (1) what employees want and need to know to do their jobs, and (2) the messages passed through the organization from top management.

To do their jobs well, and to be committed to superior performance, employees need to know:

- exactly what is expected of them; a clear definition of their specific assigned duties and the activities for which they will be held responsible and accountable.
- where their jobs fit into the total picture and why they are important.
- how their jobs affect other jobs within the organization and vice versa.
- how their mistakes affect others within and outside the organization and vice versa.
- the specific factors and criteria on which their performance will be judged, behavioral as well as technical job content; for example, service, courtesy, quality, quantity, cost, innovation, accuracy, and self-development.

- exactly how performance will be measured — quantitatively, qualitatively, and behaviorally. For example, a series of statements describe the conditions that should exist if each job responsibility has been adequately performed.
- for each area of responsibility, what constitutes below-standard, standard, or exceptional peformance, in both quantitative and qualitative terms.
- periodic progress reviews to let individuals know where they stand and how well they are doing.
- how to improve their performance and increase their contribution to the organization.
- how to develop themselves in their jobs and in the organization (employees are saying they want and need to be coached).

The second aspect of the internal communication processes has to do with the types of messages passed through the organization from top management and how employees translate these messages into their relations with customers.

Management to Employee	*Employee to Customer*
What are your problems and how can I help solve them?	How may I be of assistance to you?
We want you to know what is happening in our organization, so here is what is going on.	I am capable of helping you because I am in the know.
Each of us is the company, so we all share accountability for what happens around here.	I am empowered to help you and take pride in my ability to do so.

We treat each other with professional respect.	I have respect for you as the individual you are.
We stand behind each other's decisions and support each other.	You can count on me and my company to deliver on our promises.

Because this area is so vital to the establishment of a customer-oriented work force, we will examine each of these five messages in detail.

1. What are your problems and how can I help solve them?/How may I be of assistance to you?

The seventeen role-model organizations of the Citicorp study placed heavy emphasis on employee problem-solving procedures. There is an acute awareness that if management solves employee problems, employees solve customers' problems. It is as simple as that. Simple, but not easy.

In these companies communications between employees and management were always kept open. For example, in all McDonald's offices, everywhere, there are no doors. People are encouraged to go directly to the person anywhere in the organization who can help solve job-related problems.

In the most enlightened companies, management's interest in solving employee problems extends beyond the workplace. There has been a significant increase in employee assistance programs and day care centers, and there have been more credit unions coming into vogue.

The employee assistance program is usually made available to the employee's spouse and family members, too. Essentially, it is a referral and counseling service in which employees get confidential help in a variety of situations — psychological counseling, marriage counseling, health problems, alcohol or drug dependency, financial or legal difficulties — and for which management pays the bill. Programs like this clearly say to the employee, "We care about you."

Problem solving implies an understanding boss with a sensitivity to employees' needs and the empathy to walk in their shoes. But this does not for a moment suggest a weak or a soft boss. Most people want to work in a well-run, disciplined organization where the rules, policies, and procedures are clear, uniform, and consistently applied. Consistency and predictability are premier characteristics of effective supervisors.

McDonald's has a position called vice president for individuality. This person's main task is to keep the company small in the sense of maintaining a family atmosphere. No one should feel lost. One of the ways Mcdonald's puts its concern for the employees and their problems into action is through a series of regular employee input sessions. Here is how they work.

A cross-section of nonexempt employees from the offices and the restaurants are asked by their supervisors and managers if they wanted to sit in on an "Operation Input" session with senior management. These sessions are designed specifically to let employees tell how they perceive the company. Management says, "Tell us about your concerns, your *problems,* and what we can do to help make McDonald's a better place to work." The employees answer, and management listens and adopts as many of their suggestions as possible.

2. *We want you to know what is happening in our organization, so here is what is going on./I am capable of helping you because I am in the know.*

As an example, successful, service-oriented companies hold weekly staff meetings with all employees in small groups at all levels of the organization. At these meetings the agenda tends to be flexible. The manager or supervisor shares with the employees these types of information:

- Here is what is happening in the company — sales, profits, products, services, competition.
- Here is what is happening in other areas and other departments within the company.
- Here is what is happening in the departments that affect us and our work, and what is happening in those departments we affect.
- Are we on target in what we said we would do in budgets, costs, goals, objectives, and implementation of service policies?
- What is on your mind? An open free-for-all so that we can all share in what is happening among the several functions within a given department.

Every year, Delta and General Electric — both known for their achievements in service superiority — bring together the entire employee population in small groups. They discuss the state of the business, competition, operating trends and results, market share, new products and services, and the effectiveness of present customer service policies and practices.

At General Electric's Hotpoint Division, the general manager and those who report directly to him hold informative meetings for employees. At these meetings each functional head discusses what is happening and outlines his or her goals, objectives, contributions to business results, job security, and so on. After the presentation, the floor is open for discussion. Employees ask direct questions and are given straight answers.

Weekly staff meetings and informal employee meetings serve to ensure that employees in the organization know what is going on. The thesis is that if everyone knows what is happening throughout the organization, any chance encounter with a customer, even by a non-customer-service employee, turns out to be a benefit. The well-informed employee never says (and is never permitted to say), "I don't know" or "It's not my job." If in fact the employee does not know, that person quickly finds out or puts the customer immediately in touch with someone who can help.

As a negative example, picture your own business dealings. Have you ever been put on hold, transferred several times, and then cut off? Why was it that your call to inquire about a delivery never got through? And when you got through, how often was the message inaccurately relayed to the intended department, relayed to the wrong department, or not relayed at all?

In a more positive vein, companies that combine effective staff and employee information meetings with a sharing of all the things employees want and need to know are ensuring that their customers will get the proper service, whatever the circumstances. It is far better to err on the side of giving too much information than too little.

3. Each of us is the company, so we all share accountability for what happens around here./I am empowered to help you and take pride in my ability to do so.

To build personal accountability among all employees so they really believe that "each of us is the company," the participating companies in the Citicorp study incorporated several elements into their "people management."

As part of each employee's formal indoctrination, accountability was explained in detail, including answers to such questions as What is it? Why is it important? How does it work around here? What is my specific role in accountability to other employees and the customer?

These companies also went out of their way to reward customer-related actions beyond the call of duty and publicly praised those who set examples of personal accountability.

Most of them have a policy of commending employees for formal customer compliments, instantly routing customer feedback to the appropriate employee.

Not only are the compliments passed on, so are the less favorable comments. Any errors or customer dissatisfactions are also instantly routed back to the specific employees who caused them. Accountability for one's actions cannot be left to chance; it must be constantly refined and reinforced.

The role models also backed up decisions employees made when interacting with customers. I have seen this happen a number of times in a McDonald's restaurant where for whatever reason a customer was being unreasonable. Enlightened employees will do their utmost to please the customer but not at the expense of the employee. Both have needs that must be satisfied.

Let me tell you about one of my favorite restaurants in New York City, Akbar. I once asked the owner how he dealt with a customer complaint.

First he apologizes directly to the customer for any inconvenience. Then he talks to the waiter involved, to get his side of the story. He does not condemn the waiter; instead he requests an explanation, helps find a way to avoid repeating the problem, and finally says, "I'm sure it was a misunderstanding because you're one of my best waiters and that's not the kind of behavior you would normally demonstrate." Then he dismisses the incident, with the caution that everyone must take special pains to please the customer because "that is why we are in existence."

The Citicorp companies also have a policy of evaluating individual performance. They believe that all employees have a right to periodic progress reviews, to let them know how well they are doing. Occasionally, some people do not fully accept accountability for their actions. They make such statements as "It was the other person's fault." Those employees are dealt with within the context of a responsible grievance system that incorporates positive discipline.

As a result of these actions, companies that are truly customer-service-oriented achieve a full understanding of the scope of the individual's personal responsibility and the importance of every service transaction, and manage to have employees who take pride in their jobs and the organizations they work for.

4. We treat each other with professional respect./I have respect for you as the individual you are.

There is something called the Law of Psychological Reciprocity. It states that if I treat you with dignity and respect, you will treat me likewise. In more than thirty years of experience in industry, I have seen companies develop profound problems in employee morale through the overt lack of respect for individual employees demonstrated by thoughtless supervisors and managers. Too often this occurs in organizations with masses of low-paid employees. The ultimate effect on customer service, and thus on the company, can be disastrous.

This lack of respect for the individual manifests itself in several ways: failing to recognize and acknowledge a job well done, calling people by numbers instead of names, shouting and using abusive language, providing unclean and inadequate facilities, never saying "please" or "thank you," never making any attempt to understand the individual's point of view.

How do you suppose the employee who is not given respect is going to treat the customer? With a lack of respect, of course. If a customer is feeling belligerent or grouchy, it will not be overlooked by the employee who feels "beaten on" most of the time. But the employee who is given respect shows respect, and is more tolerant of customers who complain — rightfully or wrongfully.

In the focus group interviews mentioned earlier, more than half the 150 participants said that being treated with respect was one of the most important characteristics in an ideal boss, and that one of the major reasons they would leave a firm would be a lack of respect.

5. We stand behind each other's decisions and support each other./ You can count on me and my company to deliver on our promises.

All of us can think of times in our careers when we have had a nonsupportive boss, someone who inevitably passed the buck on to us for whatever went wrong, and worse still, took personal credit for our contributions. It is usually that same boss who never protected us, who never accepted partial responsibility for a mistake, and who made promises and never kept them. Think of a boss who could have paid you what you really deserved but decided to chisel to make himself look good, or who could have put you in for stock options but did not.

Unfortunately, there are all too many negative examples and all too few sterling role models. In my focus group interviews, once again more than half the participants wanted a boss who would support them, and they said they would quit a job if they had a nonsupportive boss.

The supportive boss fights to get the staffing and resources that you need to do your job. The supportive boss gets you the maximum pay increases and shares responsibility for anything that might go wrong. The supportive boss will not permit others to criticize you, but will personally accept the criticism for something that went wrong and will then diplomatically and conscientiously listen to your side of the story before doing anything. The serious boss does not overreact. If this boss makes a promise to you, that promise is kept.

The ideal boss has ideal employees who can be counted on to fulfill their promises to the customer because the boss fulfills his or her promises to them.

Working Conditions

Within the context of your work environment, show that you care for your employees by providing the best working conditions possible, given the limitations of your offices, factories, and facilities. Treat the lowest paid employee exactly as you yourself would like to be treated. It is as simple as that. A clean environment, a water cooler that works, climate controls, a place for privacy, a sparkling clean washroom, an inviting dining room facility — these are minimum standards.

Sometimes it is necessary to work within relatively few feet of floor space. But that space should be clean, neat, tidy, and orderly. It should be safe and as comfortable as possible. This space should give what little privacy can be afforded, even to the extent of individual partitions.

Good working conditions should go well beyond merely satisfying the legal requirements. All walls, fixtures, floors, ceilings, and furniture should be maintained in proper order and never allowed to drift into a state of dispair. There is no reason why people should feel uncomfortable with their surroundings. Never forget that if we show respect for the employee, that employee will show respect for the customer.

Compensation

We have all heard the old expression "If you pay peanuts, you get monkeys." It is not surprising that the most gifted people in this country usually go to work for those organizations that pay the most money. Money has often been cited as only the third or fourth reason people quit their jobs. It is nevertheless a powerful motivator if applied properly. As organizations learn to link their reward systems to performance more effectively, money can become a super motivator.

To use compensation as a motivator, organizations must not neglect either aspect: compensation must be both externally competitive and internally equitable. This is important because employees measure their self-worth in terms of what they earn versus what the market pays.

The Public Affairs Foundation took a national poll in 1983 among hourly paid workers. They found that only 22 percent of the workers saw any connection between how hard they worked and how much they were paid. As a consequence, 73 percent of those workers exerted less than full effort. In a real pay-for-performance system, workers should participate in identifying the measures on which their pay will be based.

An employee who feels improperly compensated will feel cheated. Cheated employees will not fully support the organization's goals. The commitment to service superiority that organizations seek will not occur when employees feel that management is exploiting them or holding back. Exploitation produces a negative attitude, which in turn influences how well employees meet one another's needs as well as the needs of customers.

A similar negative effect can be produced if employees feel they are improperly compensated in relation to one another or to comparable jobs within the organization. If "A" produces more than "B" working in a comparable job, "A" logically expects to get paid more than "B."

I marvel at the naiveté of organizations that fail to perceive what happens when all employees get the same annual birthday increase of 5 percent. The best performers are driven out and the worst performers are encouraged to stay.

In these situations, morale is usually quite poor. It is the customer who suffers, but when he subsequently takes his business elsewhere — as he will — the company suffers more.

Policy and Administration

The best-managed companies have simple, clear personnel policies, and administer them consistently. My own philosophy is that policies should be relatively few, thoroughly communicated, and rigidly enforced. An exception all too soon becomes a rule, and employees are quick to pick up on a manager's inconsistencies.

Solid, well-thought-through, basic, understandable personnel policies, applied uniformly with consistency and objectivity, serve to assure fair and consistent treatment throughout the organization. The rewards for exemplary service behavior are also administered consistently with good policies.

For example, take a disciplinary policy. If one supervisor ignores or excuses employees' absences or tardiness while another holds to the letter of the policy, this inconsistency in administration will penalize some while letting others get off the hook scot-free. This will translate directly into inconsistency in customer service. Policies serve to protect both employees and the customer. They help to provide a clearly defined employment contract.

Typical policies, often formalized in a supervisor's manual, will include time off, vacations, holidays, shift differentials, pay and incentives, progressive discipline, and work assignments.

Job Security

One need only look at what happens to productivity and customer service after a layoff to recognize fully the consequences of insecurity. All the participating companies in the Citicorp study clearly recognized that to gain loyalty from their work force, they first had to demonstrate loyalty *to* that work force.

Loyalty on the part of the organization means that the work

force is kept intact in bad times as well as good. The lifetime job security provided by Japanese companies is well known. While I strongly believe it would be unwise to try to emulate the Japanese culture, we can certainly learn a thing or two from them.

In this country the top companies within their respective industries generally try to have a no-layoff policy. They also happen to be the tops in customer service, and this is not by accident. Just look at McDonald's, IBM, and Delta Airlines. Loyalty begets loyalty.

Mind you, these firms are not soft. They are tough and they are demanding. They have high expectations and stringent performance standards, but they get in return what they give. And the employee does the same to the customer.

To provide job security, for example, McDonald's uses a variety of outside suppliers and a mostly temporary work force in its restaurants. Natural attrition is preplanned. For those who choose to stay and build a career with McDonald's, many of whom started out as part-time crew members, the future is secure and the growth opportunity is phenomenal. Promotion from within is a way of life.

Achievement

The overwhelming majority of people who come to work want very much to do the very best job humanly possible. But when people feel underutilized, they become restless and dissatisfied. When their suggestions are ignored, they retire on the job and stop using their minds. They virtually disappear into their job descriptions.

Each of us has a built-in mechanism called the "need to achieve." If we are deprived of that opportunity by a boss who fails to delegate, showing evidence of mistrust, we adopt an "I don't care" attitude and then we permit that boss to hang himself.

We often hear that most work forces can increase their productivity by 40 percent or more. A research study of American workers by Theodore Berry and Associates revealed that both white- and blue-collar workers are idle somewhere between 40 and 50 percent of their time. I believe that a major cause of this lost productivity is that the typical employee is underutilized, improperly trained, or both. The fact is that most people want to achieve, but the way they are managed either turns them off or prevents them from doing so.

Organizations that set high levels of expectation for the work force consistently turn in better results in all areas, including customer service. David Cherrington, associate professor of organizational behavior at Brigham Young University, surveyed hundreds of workers in more than fifty companies. He found that managers who establish high levels of expectation got higher levels of productivity. In one particular study, supervisors were told to communicate either high, low, or no performance standards. The highest performance rates were achieved by the groups whose superiors expected and communicated high standards of performance.

American workers, I firmly believe, have lost their basic work ethic. The environment management creates makes it difficult for the individual to achieve. Too often, conformity is rewarded, not creativity. And it is creativity that leads to achievement.

Recognition for Achievement

If supervisors and managers could do just one thing to achieve customer service superiority, it would be to learn to give recognition. Public recognition for exceptional performance in customer service sets a tone for the entire organization. It makes the individual who is recognized grow ten feet tall. It stimulates others in a healthy, competitive way to want to do likewise.

In the focus groups mentioned earlier, more than 80 percent of the participants felt they were not sufficiently recognized for their achievements. The same percentage said if more recognition were not forthcoming, they would seriously consider leaving the company.

Somewhere I read that the best reward for high achievement is to give the individual the opportunity to achieve more. That opportunity translates into broader job responsibilities and possibly promotion, which is one form of recognition, and it should also be accompanied by lots of public recognition as reflected in the reward system. But do not stop there. Also put it in the individual's paycheck. Reward achievement with money as well as praise and more opportunity to achieve.

Even if your system does not provide for differential rewards, there are ways to reward your best service employees who achieve the highest standards. You can give them time off with full pay, extra carfare, free lunches, and lots of recognition. Otherwise how can you possibly continue to maintain their loyalty, support, and motivation as a service team?

In *Real Bosses Don't Say Thank You* Ellen Nevins gives these tongue-in-cheek guidelines for giving feedback:

- Give all feedback at once, usually at the time of the annual appraisal. (Make sure it's a total surprise to the individual.)
- Don't tell anyone they're doing a good job. (They probably know it anyway.)
- If they're not doing a good job, they probably don't care anyway. (So why give suggestions for improvement?)
- Don't praise very highly or give much credit. (The individual might expect a raise.)
- If you cannot escape giving praise, make sure it's not in

front of the individual's peer group. (It might demoralize and demotivate others.)

- On the other hand, there's real value in "chewing out" the person who has made a mistake in front of the peers. (The person who's being read the riot act will avoid the behavior that caused this in order to avoid being embarrassed publicly again.)

Involvement

The basic principle behind quality circles, performance teams, and participative management is involvement. People feel good about themselves when they become totally immersed and involved in the business, and everyone connected with that business receives added value and satisfaction. If the workplace and the management style are such that all employees are involved in as many aspects of the business as possible, a sense of ownership and stewardship is fostered. The customer ultimately benefits.

As an example, the Digital Equipment Corporation in Enfield, Connecticut, gives employees total responsibility for producing a quality product. A nontraditional floor plan helps employees to learn all aspects of the manufacturing process. They build the complete product from start to finish.

This system is similar to McDonald's, where the hourly employees literally run the operation, from opening the store, to mastering each work station, to closing at night. It significantly increases the sense of ownership.

At Digital Equipment the system of product ownership has increased employee motivation, decreased throughput time by 40 percent, and doubled the number of flawless modules produced. In the eighteen-person performance teams, each individual is expected to perform all twenty-seven functions required to manufacture a board. That person will gather raw materials, build, test, and ship the module. There are no time clocks, no assembly lines, no supervisors, no quality control inspectors, and no guards. Employees choose their own hours and plan their own schedules. Team members interface directly with the customer.

This concept has been successful because of employee ownership and responsibility. All employees put their initals on the products and say, "I did that." In similar fashion, employees at Weyco put their names on products they make. It signifies a sense of pride, a sense of ownership.

Participation

People make the best decisions when they use the collective wisdom of the group. It is only natural for people to want to participate in decisions that affect them. Participation reduces resistance to change and gives employees a sense of ownership.

Part of the psychological contract that should be made with every employee is, "We will first discuss with you any decisions that affect you directly in your work. We both need and want your ideas." When this input is sought and given, it should be used, otherwise a large part of that benefit is lost. Employees feel management is not serious if they do not adopt at least some of their suggestions. But when employee suggestions are adopted, management's expectations are surpassed. Capital projects inevitably achieve their intended results earlier than anticipated.

One of the dairies I work with on a regular basis was extremely pressed for space. They needed a new separator, but they were not sure where to place it or what it would do to the work flow and the individuals involved. So they simply asked all the employees affected by the separator to come up with a solution on its location and the impact on work flow.

The employees enthusiastically tackled the project and came up with a solution. No production was lost in the process. More important, the customers continued to receive the excellent service they had been accustomed to.

Advancement

Most people want to get ahead. Life becomes more meaningful when we have something to look forward to each day at work. Each job advancement becomes a new thrill, a new opportunity. When we no longer perceive opportunities personally and professionally, we quit. And when we quit who is it that suffers? The customer, through poor service.

In my focus groups, 75 percent of the participants said they would leave the company if they felt there was no opportunity to advance. Advancement does not necessarily imply frequent promotion. But it does imply the development of new skills and abilities. In a period of relatively flat growth, people can be given special assignments, such as participation in a task force, or training for specialization or job enlargement.

Creative management of human resources in today's turbulent times means paying more attention to the needs of the work force, so that the work force in turn will pay more attention to the needs of the customer. This will create that perceptible difference between you and your competition.

BUILDING THE CUSTOMER-ORIENTED WORK FORCE

❏ *Recruiting, Hiring, and Orienting Employees*

To excel in customer service, an organization must have employees — from top to bottom — who share a commitment to providing superior service. A company can ensure this commitment by helping employees see that service superiority is in their own best interests. One of the things the highly successful service-oriented companies identified in the Citicorp study had in common was that they took every conceivable step to make sure employees understood that their personal job security was totally dependent on the firm's ability to satisfy the customers and make them want to come back.

Building a work force with this kind of commitment to customer service is a full process. The process starts with establishing clear corporate values of service superiority, then recruiting and hiring people who share those values and continually reinforcing those values, from the first day of orientation all the way to the retirement party.

❑ Transferring Service Awareness to Employees

The importance of the individual is constantly stressed. The need for service superiority is sold to the individual employee in terms of what it does for that employee. McDonald's, for instance, effectively sells what is essentially a minimum-wage job, with no tipping, by emphasizing the tremendous benefits and personal satisfaction that come from serving the customer. Each potential employee is told: "In serving the customer, you will gain the following benefits":

- You will learn important skills, and they will help you succeed in life regardless of whatever you choose to do after McDonald's.
- You are special and you want the satisfaction of knowing that your work helps others — other employees and customers as well as yourself.
- Whatever you want from life you can get because you will learn how to motivate others — employees and customers.
- You learn how to serve customers so that they will want to come back. You discover things about yourself and capabilities you did not know you possessed.
- You get a clear idea of how a system runs and of all the little things that add up to the satisfaction of the customer and the crew — primarily yourself.

McDonald's continues to tell its individual crew people, "You can take charge of your life. McDonald's can help you do it." It provides a lesson in basic economics in terms of how the employee fits in: "Your job, your pay, and your advancement will depend on how well the customers are served, because the company's overall profitability is tied to that." It is fun to be part of a winning team.

McDonald's continues to emphasize awareness of the need for service superiority by talking about the beneficial effects to the entire economy if it sold more hamburgers. More jobs would be created in a variety of business sectors. The end result is a higher standard of living for everyone.

❑ Hiring the Right People

Customer service superiority begins with whom we hire, how we hire them, and how we bring them into our organization. A training consultant recently told me, "If you hire bums and give them to me, I will give you back trained bums." The idea, of course, is not to hire bums but to hire the kind of people who will want to give good service.

During the interview process itself, the organization's values are emphasized. The importance of customer service is made clear. After the open-ended questions are asked by the interviewer, the candidate is told what behaviors are rewarded and what behaviors are unacceptable. This is where the teaching process begins.

The best way to "select in" those with the predisposed customer-service orientation (and to screen out those who are deficient in this area) is through what is called behaviorally oriented interviewing. The goal of the interview is to select the candidates who have, in their life and work experiences, already demonstrated a service orientation. Behaviorally oriented interviewing is used to predict how a candidate will behave in your job and your organization. It features a patterned interview, which uses a candidate's past job-related behavior to predict future success.

Some of the behavioral characteristics that constitute a service orientation include oral communication skills, cooperation and teamwork, problem-solving, decision making, sensitivity and concern for others, dependability, judgment, enthusiasm, high energy level, flexibility, and adaptability. A patterned interview will reveal these characteristics.

A patterned interview is a highly structured format during which candidates talk more than 70 percent of the time, describing their previous work experiences in response to open-ended questions. It uses past job behavior to predict future behavior. It is based on two fundamental premises. First, most newly hired employees want to succeed and, from a technical perspective, are able to do the job. Second, most failures spring not from a lack of technical competence but from the individual's inability to adjust his or her behavior to conform to the organization's norms. Hence the patterned interview. It pinpoints the behaviors necessary for a person to succeed in the company. The format for the patterned interview is based on eight to ten specific behavioral characteristics for the particular position. Once the job-related behaviors are identified, three to five questions are developed for each, to determine whether the candidate possesses these characteristics and to what degree.

The patterned interview works because everyone involved in the selection process is comparing apples and apples. The advantages of this system are that it reduces the risk of poor selection decisions, "selects in" those who will share your values, saves training time and money, minimizes the risk of failure and performance problems, is judged to be legally defensible, and saves the manager's time.

Suppose, for example, you are hiring a vice president of sales and one of the major responsibilities is to train, develop, and motivate the sales force. The important job-related behavioral characteristic here is people development. Here are four representative questions designed to get at an individual's skills in people development.

- How do you identify people with potential for promotion? Specify your criteria.
- What are some of the things you do to develop your people?
- What do you get out of a performance appraisal review and feedback session? For your direct reports? For yourself as a manager?
- What do you do with the subordinate who does things contrary to your direction? How do you measure the effectiveness of this approach?

Imagine that three individuals in the company are involved in the selection process. Each asks one of these questions and then they compare notes. A great deal of the subjectivity is removed because all candidates can be compared on the same criteria.

Other job-related behavioral characteristics for a successful sales manager could include problem analysis and problem-solving, oral communications, organization and planning, quality of work standards, decision making, delegation, administration, interviewing, and counseling. Specific questions could be developed that would bring these characteristics to light.

While many of the job-related behaviors necessary for success are similar from one business to another, the traits should be customized for a given company. For example, one company might place a premium on a high level of tolerance for frustration and stress, whereas another company in the same industry might put an equally high premium on decisiveness and action.

Want to improve your batting average and reduce the failure rate among new hires? Try a patterned interview. When we introduced behavioral interviewing at McDonald's, we reduced management trainee turnover from more than 50 percent to less than 30 percent.

❑ The Importance of Orientation

If you are fortunate enough to lure potentially good employees to join your organization, please do not turn them off on the first day or in the first week or in the first month.

An effective orientation program may well mean the difference between success or failure for the new employee. For better or for worse, the orientation will leave an immediate and lasting impression. The successful orientation process will result in fewer mistakes, improved customer service, higher levels of productivity, and more harmonious employee relations. It welcomes the employee to a warm, friendly, caring environment. The employee who feels welcomed and important will make the customer feel welcomed and important.

Most of the service leaders in the Citicorp study treat the employee's first day on the job as a cause for a two-way celebration. It is in those early stages that the individual should be made to feel comfortable, as well as familiar with whatever is necessary to understand and perform the job efficiently. This is the vital first step in integrating the employee's needs with those of the organization and consequently those of the customer.

A successful orientation process should be customized to fit the particular needs of a given organization. However, there are certain characteristics that most successful orientation processes have in common. Responsibilities and accountabilities are fixed and clearly understood by all those involved in the orientation process, from the personnel manager, to the immediate supervisor, to the "buddy" assigned to teach the new employee. The new employee is made to feel secure and welcome in the new and unfamiliar environment. He or she learns all that is needed to perform the job well. There is ample, planned opportunity to meet the supervisory staff and other employees, and the employee is given a basic understanding of the company, its history, its values, its traditions, its business, its customers, and its reward system. The new person is told of the performance expectations and specific duties in precise detail as well as where and how to get help and how this particular job relates to other jobs in the organization. The process is spread out over a period of time to avoid information overload. For instance, after a week or two, the employee may be invited back in to discuss how things are going. Full information on pay, benefits, hours, working conditions, terms, and conditions of employment is provided, and opportunities for training, learning, and potential advancement are explained early on. Policies, rules, and regulations are described in detail; "how we do things around here" is made clear. Written materials are provided for subsequent study and review and reference. Checklists are used to assure that all topics in the orientation process are covered, and feedback is solicited from the employee, by an independent third party, on the effectiveness and thoroughness of the entire process.

In the Citicorp role model companies, orientation is taken very seriously. A lot of money is spent to recruit the right people, so they invest more in assimilating the individual to the organization. Orientation is spread out over two or three weeks in time and often divided into three different sessions.

1. *First Session*
   a. Traditions program: who we are, what we represent, how we do business, our company values, our common

language; explanation and discussion of why we are in business, who our competitors are, who our customers are, and how we treat them.
   b. A complete tour of the office facilities and plant operations.
2. *Second Session*
   a. Orientation to the employee's particular division, department, and function. It includes how decisions are made, how problems are solved, and what behavior is rewarded. Here the training emphasizes the close teamwork needed to produce a product or deliver a quality service.
   b. Training includes the need for interdependence and teamwork along with the nature of the work, the job itself, the challenges, and the opportunities.
3. *Third Session*
   a. Orientation to the employee's specific job.
   b. A review of the job description, performance standards, expectations, and mutual responsibilities.
   c. How the person's work and mistakes affect others in the work unit and beyond.
   d. Why this particular job is important and exactly how it contributes to business results.

ESTABLISHING AND MAINTAINING HIGH STANDARDS FOR CUSTOMER SERVICE

When companies strive for a high level of customer service, it soon becomes clear that it is not enough to say, "Be nice to the customer." Eventually you have to define just what "nice" means. Goodness in one's heart is no guarantee of quality.

Employees need to understand what they will be held accountable for and what standards their performance will be measured against. Two things are involved; they work in concert, and both are needed: a precise written job description, delineating the exact areas each employee is responsible for, and a detailed set of performance standards for each job, setting out as specifically as possible the behavior expected in all elements of the job.

❏ Importance of Job Descriptions

All too often, effort is wasted simply because employees do not fully understand just exactly what they are responsible and accountable for. So instead they spend a great deal of time in defensive maneuvering.

The boss often assumes — incorrectly — that the employee knows exactly what to do and how to do it, even the exact sequence in order of priority. Quite the opposite is true. It must be written down or it will not happen.

Of the 152 people interviewed in the focus group sessions mentioned earlier, an astonishing 70 percent said they were unclear what the basis was for measuring their own performance. At the top of their wish list was a clear, well-defined job description with meaningful, precise, well-communicated performance standards.

The same phenomenon applies right on up through the line. You would be amazed to know how many middle and senior managers are not aware of the standards for their jobs, the impact they are expected to make, or the basis on which they will be measured.

In a medium-sized midwestern company where I served as personnel director, we initiated a job description process. We found that anywhere from one to three people each claimed responsibility and accountability for exactly the same job factors. A few people noted two or more direct reporting relationships. And a number of jobs were nonjobs — a crutch for someone who could not perform. They included such titles as liaison, coordinator, and assistant.

At McDonald's everybody had a written job description — all restaurant employees and all managers. The job description served as a tool for establishing performance standards, setting goals, coaching performance, and conducting appraisal reviews and discussions. The job description for restaurant employees incorporated customer service standards to ensure the achievement of the organization's objectives in quality, service, cleanliness, and value to the customer. Job descriptions for management incorporated additional areas of responsibility and reflected the same behavior characteristics that were explored in the interviewing process. Ultimately, managers are expected to help establish and reinforce service performance standards for all customer-contact employees.

A good job description becomes the basis for many critical human resource functions. Specifically, a good job description provides a foundation for the following:

- compensation
- selection
- orientation
- induction
- training
- establishing standards of performance
- setting new goals and objectives
- performance coaching
- progress reviews
- performance appraisal and review
- employee development
- planned advancement
- job posting
- career pathing

To show you one possible format, a sample job description is included in Appendix A.

To put together a job description and begin the process of establishing service performance standards, consider the following steps. First, ask all who report to you to list the six to eight major responsibilities of their position by priority of importance. Then you do the same, for each employee. Exchange papers. Now you have begun to provide the basis for a clear understanding of the job responsibilities, accountability for business results, and priorities. Normally, this exercise results in two or three items on one person's list that do not appear on the other's. Small wonder that there is so much misunderstanding about standards!

Next, get the individual to describe briefly the exact condition that should exist (quantitatively or qualitatively) if each of those six or eight major job responsibilities is being performed to standard, above-standard, or below-standard level. Get your employees to put themselves in the position of the customer: How would they like to be treated? You have now started the second step: using the job description to establish performance standards.

□ Performance Standards

Mary Kay Ash, chairperson of Mary Kay Cosmetics, has said that many companies talk about excellence, but until they establish measurable and obtainable standards, employees will not have a target to aim at. That is what performance standards are all about.

Performance standards describe in detail for each position and each individual responsibility within that job exactly what conditions will exist if service superiority is to become a reality. And that includes accidental, happenstance encounters with customers by non-customer-contact employees. Nothing is left to chance.

Just as an illustration, let us look at the training and service standards of an hourly employee at McDonald's. The cashier at the counter is taught six very exact steps for taking a customer's order. For each of those six steps there are precise behavioral service standards. Take a look at breakfast.

Step 1: Greet the Customer.

Standards: 1. Wish the customer a pleasant "good morning" and do so with a cheerful smile.

2. When asking for the order do so courteously. Please give a friendly greeting to let your customers know you are there to help them.

3. Call regular customers by name. It says to them, "You are important." It adds the dimension of warmth to an otherwise cold business transaction.

Step 2: Take the Order.

Standards: 1. Register the order into the cash register as the customer is giving it.

2. Be thoroughly familiar with all items on the menu.

3. Answer each question the customer may ask about ingredients, food freshness, content, and handling times.

4. If you receive orders for items we do not carry, suggest a similar or related menu item. Do not say, "We don't carry that particular product."

5. Be particularly helpful with detailed explanations to new customers and they will become repeat customers.

6. If a customer orders an item after the breakfast period has ended explain politely that this practice is necessary to provide quality service and fresh food.

7. Suggest only one additional item to your customer, "How about a nice hot Danish to go with that steaming hot cup of coffee?"

8. Accept special orders graciously.

9. It is okay to substitute or ask for additional portions but make the appropriate price adjustment.

Step 3: Assemble the Order.

Standards: 1. The first thing to do is find out whether the order is to go or to eat in.
2. Follow precisely the prescribed sequence steps: cold drinks first, hot drinks next, and food last.
3. Follow the detailed instructions concerning how to pack the order, what size bag to use, and whether to include a plastic knife, a fork, or a jelly packet.

Step 4: Present the Order.

Standards: 1. Standards cover the exact positioning of each item on the tray for both appearance and convenience.
2. Present the tray with all the items neatly arranged. An attractive appearance is an important part of customer service. It says to the customer that you take pride in your job, your company, your products, and your abilities to please that customer.
3. A customer should never have to reach for the order.
4. State the amount and ask for payment courteously.

Step 5: Request Payment.

Standards: 1. Repeat the amount of the sale and the amount you received in a crisp, clear voice.
2. Place all bills on the cash register drawer.
3. Count out the change carefully.
4. Count the bills and the change directly into the customer's hand.

Step 6: Thank You and Call Again.

Standards: 1. Thank every customer and invite that person to come back to McDonald's.
    2. When you have a breakfast customer, be sure to wish that person a happy day.
    3. Let the individual know you would be personally happy to see him or her come back again.

One of the real benefits of precise and exact behavioral performance standards is that they create in the employee's mind an acute sense of customer awareness. Thus the importance of the customer is emphasized and reemphasized, with each and every transaction.

As an hourly paid crew chief advances into a management trainee role at McDonald's, customer awareness takes on new dimensions of meaning. As a crew person, that individual was trained in all aspects of customer awareness, everything having to do with quality, service, cleanliness, and value. As a manager, that individual is now taught how to make additional decisions that directly relate to customer satisfaction in such areas as handling customer complaints, dealing with injuries to customers, and managing unruly individuals or groups. For all these areas, too, there are very precise performance standards.

All management trainees are given assignments in these areas. When these assignments are completed, they are evaluated by their supervisors. Here they build on a strong foundation of standards for customer satisfaction. Here are a few examples.

A Customer Complains about an Order.

Standards: 1. Apologize for any possible mistake.
    2. Use your judgment in replacing the order. Err on the side of the customer.

3. Do not ask for more money.
4. Show concern in your remarks and in your approach.
5. Make sure the customer is satisfied before you walk away.

A Customer Complains about a Foreign Object in the Food.

Standards: 1. Apologize for any inconvenience it might have caused.
2. Ask the customer if you may have the object.
3. Write down the customer's name, address, and phone number.
4. Offer to replace the item.
5. Offer to contact a physician and do so if the person agrees.
6. Tell the individual you will report this to the proper company authorities.
7. Say nothing that might even *begin* to imply the company could be at fault.
8. Complete insurance papers and notify the insurance carrier.

This same meticulous attention to detail, to precise standards of behavior, is also applied to such management concerns as customer injury on the premises, damage to store property, disturbances by individuals or groups, and complaints regarding short change.

To ensure that the standards were carefully understood and internalized, management trainees are thoroughly examined and evaluated. After they read the appropriate module instructions form, they discuss it with the manager. Then they are required to take a test covering all the material for that particular module. This includes completing certain specific objectives. For example, they have to answer a series of open-ended questions to measure understanding and application of the correct behavioral performance standards for helping a customer file an insurance claim.

The actual test of knowledge, ability, and understanding comes from observation by the manager and discussion with the trainee. Observations include the actual handling of, for instance, three customer complaints. Finally the manager trainee, as part of the normal job routine, is asked to convey to the crew, by word and deed, the total importance of customer satisfaction.

What do McDonald's and world-class hotels have in common? An emphasis on service. For example, here is a sample list of performance standards for all managers in a hotel chain.

1. *Communication with Guests.* Accepts feedback on performance, solicits suggestions for improvement; exercises aggressive hospitality; acknowledges and takes initiative to solve guest problems; delivers service in a friendly, professional manner.

2. *Communication with Subordinates.* Provides effective, timely information to subordinates; solicits input on problems and suggestions for improvement; accepts feedback on performance.

3. *Communication with Superiors.* Provides effective, timely information and feedback to superiors; solicits input on problems and suggestions for improvement; accepts feedback on performance.

4. *Communication with Other Departments.* Provides effective, timely information and feedback to other departments; solicits input on problems and suggestions for improvement; accepts feedback on performance.

5. *Conducting Meetings.* Prepares agenda prior to meetings; adheres to and completes agenda; holds meetings when

needed and as required; encourages participation and facilitates discussion appropriately.

6. *Self-Development.* Identifies own developmental needs with superior; establishes, actively pursues, and reaches specific self-development goals; updates goals on an ongoing basis.

7. *Subordinate Training and Development.* Identifies subordinates' specific training needs with subordinates' input; develops skills and knowledge of subordinates on a timely and ongoing basis; follows up to ensure desired growth is being achieved.

8. *Ongoing Critique.* Gives ongoing, timely feedback (including praise) to subordinates about their performance; creates an environment conducive to hearing and responding to subordinates' problems.

9. *Counseling.* Addresses specific problems with subordinates as soon after the fact as possible; seeks their input; develops plan with them to solve problems; follows up with feedback and encouragement to ensure resolution of problems.

10. *Discipline.* Acts fairly on discipline matters; adheres to disciplinary policies; follows and encourages use of the Guarantee of Fair Treatment.

11. *Subordinate Evaluation.* Objectively evaluates subordinates' performance against standards and goals; discusses performance in a manner that effectively fosters improvement; evaluates paperwork in a timely manner.

12. *Following Directions.* Effectively carries out instructions of superiors; acts on suggestions and feedback from superiors; meets deadlines.

13. *Delegation.* Delegates appropriate responsibility and authority to subordinates for specific tasks, decisions, and follow-up; provides clear and complete instructions; states expectations precisely; uses subordinates' capabilities most effectively.

14. *Motivation.* Encourages and inspires subordinates to accomplish tasks; creates enthusiasm and positive work environments for subordinates; rewards performance; sets good example.
15. *Teamwork.* Coordinates work of subordinates to ensure that appropriate attention is paid to highest priority tasks; encourages and generates collective effort within department and with other departments to work for common goals.
16. *Goal-Setting.* Sets precise, measurable, achievable goals for department and with subordinates, goals that are realistic and challenging and that meet the most critical business needs; sets specific intermediate action steps, with due dates, to accomplish goals; prioritizes goals appropriately.
17. *Identifying Problems.* Recognizes early signs of changing conditions and potential problems; analyzes causes for problems using all available and appropriate resources (including subordinates).
18. *Solving Problems.* Calls on appropriate people to help identify and creatively explore alternative solutions, select best solutions, and implement solutions in a timely manner; assists others in solving problems; follows up to ensure problems are resolved; takes corrective actions when necessary.
19. *Productivity.* Achieves quantity and quality standards while maintaining minimum labor costs; understands and effectively uses forecasting and labor management policies, systems, and procedures.

EFFECTIVE
EMPLOYEE TRAINING

❏ *Making a Visible Difference for the Customer*

Superiority in customer service does not just happen by chance. When the right things happen from a customer's point of view, it is a combination of doing many things right and doing the right thing on a day-to-day basis.

People will do the right things, and do things right, if they are properly trained to do so. Employees who are well trained produce superior products, which in turn require a minimum of service. And training is continuously repeated to reinforce the learning and maintain the desired behavior.

As Phillip Crosby has explained in *Quality Without Tears,* in an overall sense, education has three phases: executive education, in which senior management learns its role; management education, in which those who must implement the process learn how to do it; and an employee education system, in which all the employees of the company learn their roles, and including workshops in which those with special functions learn how to contribute to service superiority.

All of the seventeen role model companies from the Citicorp study endorsed the philosophy of training. Each made major investments — often 1 or 2 percent of gross sales — in formal, *ongoing* training programs. It is an investment they cannot afford to pass up.

In a broad sense, all the leaders' training programs focus on developing and maintaining skills in three general areas: job-related skills, positive attitudes toward customers and co-workers, and overall company knowledge. All three are closely interrelated, and all pertain directly to the achievement and maintenance of service superiority.

All employees are taught exactly what is meant by service superiority and exactly how to achieve it. Through multiple teaching media, including audiovisual and personal training, the values of teamwork and interdependence are emphasized as vital links in the chain of service superiority. All employees are taught how their work and their mistakes affect others and vice versa. They are taught that while the customer picks up the tab, it is ultimately the employee who suffers and pays.

To emphasize the importance of training, let me tell you about two situations I am acquainted with. One concerns a large publishing and printing operation that built a very sophisticated and very expensive — $100 million plus — automated factory. Two years later the plant was running at less than 70 percent efficiency.

On close inspection it was discovered that only $50,000 had been allotted to training. Middle managers, supervisors, and employees were unable to cope with the multitude of changes in working relationships brought on by the new technology. The end result was that many customers did not get their magazines and newspapers on time. The training budget was increased to $250,000, and within six months 90 percent capacity had been achieved.

In Central Falls, Rhode Island, GTE Lighting Products had just two months to open a plant that had been purchased from Corning. Comprehensive training played a major role in this transition. The trainers were hourly employees who had expertise in the production of fluorescent tubes. They all had a stake in seeing that newly hired employees did well.

In close cooperation with the training administrator, the hourly trainers wrote the training manuals. They then acted out the step-by-step instructions for each operation and videotaped the correct way to do things. Afterward, each newly hired employee was assigned to one of the hourly paid trainers for at least six to ten hours of classroom work and practice experience on the shop floor.

The sequence of training was to study the manual, watch the videotape, and practice steps on the shop floor. Then the new employee was videotaped, and the trainer and the employee reviewed the tape and decided what changes were necessary. Then the employee practiced again, until it was perfect. When the employee was ready, the trainer "signed off" to certify readiness.

GTE plans to expand its training program in every area because it brings an employee's productivity up to standard more quickly than just sending the new person out to the line operation.

There are other benefits from this training. Employee turnover is minimal, and product quality is high. Because the skills were taught properly up front, quality was excellent from the start. This also meant virtually no customer service problems.

❑ When Does Training Start and Where Does It End?

The seventeen service leaders begin training during the selection process itself and continue right on through an individual's retirement. If service superiority is to be achieved and then maintained, training must be a lifelong process, as shown in Figure 1.

In the role model companies, just about everybody goes to school for at least a full week every year to reinforce and maintain those desired behaviors once established. Every supervisor at General Electric and IBM, for instance, goes to school to make sure that slippage does not occur.

In *Vanguard Management*, James O'Toole identifies lifelong career training as one of the major features that characterize superiority in service and productivity. Among the firms he describes are Johnson & Johnson, Hewlett-Packard, Motorola, and John Deere. Coincidentally, the firms he applauds for excellence in training also lead their respective industries in productivity, cost effectiveness, profitability, and overall management effectiveness.

Here are some of the considerations that go into the service leaders' ongoing training programs:

FIGURE 1. THE PROFESSIONALIZATION PATH FOR SERVICE PERSONNEL

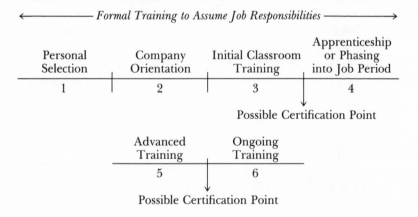

- Employees are taught what questions to ask their supervisors.
- Supervisors are taught how to respond to those questions.
- Clear expectations — which are considered just as important as skills training — are set forth.
- To ensure uniformity and consistency, all formal training is centrally developed but locally implemented.
- There is a full menu of management training in such subject areas as performance management, human resource motivation, and effective supervision.
- Supervisory training programs are mandatory — at least one full week every year for each supervisor.
- Training provides a constant service focus for employees. It emphasizes that there is no single panacea. Ongoing training is necessary to maintain service standards.
- Training is used extensively to motivate and sustain service attitudes in behind-the-scene (back-room) employees by stressing how their jobs affect customers indirectly.
- All heavy phone users take a course in "Putting a Smile in Your Voice."
- Training is used to create teamwork and team spirit. Its messages are:
    We are one big team and one happy family.
    Everyone is a problem identifier or fixer — not a problem creator.
    We are proud of our esprit de corps.
    We are all in the service business.
    All departments have customers and all of us are customers of other departments.

A significant part of the training effort teaches all employees, supervisors, and managers the value of communicating openly and the skills to do so. Later on in this chapter we will examine some communications skills workshops.

❏ The Example of One Industry

The extensive use that is made of training in the fast food industry illustrates its importance. The industry today is struggling with decreasing productivity, intense competition for employees and for business, and increased turnover. Industry executives and restaurant experts are looking to employee training as a solution to these problems. In the highly competitive fast food service business, formal training programs are viewed as a matter of survival.

A survey conducted by the restaurant trade publication *Restaurants and Institutions* made it clear that training budgets are on the increase in restaurants and hotels. Seventy-five organizations responded to the survey; sixteen operate their own training centers. Food service training will continue to expand.

Incidentally, there is a way for smaller organizations that do not have their own training facilities to participate in excellent training programs. Professional and trade associations frequently offer their members the advantage of pooled resources. For a relatively modest fee, top-flight training is available to those organizations that want to make their businesses more profitable from a service perspective.

As organizations struggle to create a perceptible difference in service, they find it is not necessary to reinvent the wheel. They need merely look to see what others have done, and follow their examples. The best example I know of is McDonald's.

Training at McDonald's is intensive and progressive. For each work station, there is a precise series of steps. Each employee

- reads the specifics about the particular work station.
- watches a precise audiovisual on the assigned work station.

- receives additional personal instruction in a private or semi-private setting from the training coordinator.
- is assigned a buddy (a star/mentor) to help out. The mentor actually works the station, explains it in detail, and watches the trainee go through it. Accuracy is stressed before speed, and the objectives of the station are spelled out in detail.
- takes a basic knowledge test, oral and written.
- works the station alone but under observation and with ongoing feedback and progress reviews.
- receives a performance evaluation against specific standards and station objectives.
- moves on to the next station and repeats the process. This gives flexibility and versatility to the work force.

The continuous repetition does not allow one to forget. Mistakes are corrected positively and diplomatically but immediately. Psychologically, the employees want to prove that they are up to the task. Each detailed step has a detailed standard of performance attached to it (see Chapter 4).

For each of the six steps at the counter, training is detailed in huge operating manuals with lesson plans, specific audio-visuals, basic and advanced verbal and written tests, and objectives for each station. Take something relatively simple like making a shake for a customer. It goes something like this. First, the new employee reads the manual that introduces the particular station. He or she watches the appropriate videotape and takes notes, then discusses the tape with the crew trainer (an hourly paid employee). The trainee and the trainer read and discuss the job procedure card, and then the crew trainer starts the floor training program. The trainer performs, with precision, a large number of steps, some ten or fifteen, all of them necessary to make a fine shake — not too thick or too thin, not too heavy or too light. The trainee is then allowed to make a shake following this step-by-step sequence. He or she is carefully supervised during the entire process, and mistakes are corrected. Next comes the basic shake test. The trainee is under observation until all the steps are mastered.

After trainees learn the basic steps involved in delivering accuracy and quality, it is time to get up speed. When I took the training course, a young teenager was my mentor and store trainer. "Bob, it's easy," she said. "After you've taken the order, the secret in assembling it and drawing the shake is to take two steps to your left and pirouette to your right." And she was right. Using her advice, I was able to increase my speed quickly.

At Hamburger University, McDonald's teaches the value of devoting time and personal attention to crew training and discusses how it affects employees' enthusiasm and involvement in the business. And McDonald's is not alone. It no longer exclusively owns these secrets. The same meticulous attention to detail through rigorous training is being done by most fast food restaurants, hotels, banks, airlines, auto rental agencies, hospitals, and retail organizations in general. The competition is tough out there, and all are attempting to create a competitive edge by establishing that perceptible difference in the customer's mind.

❑ How Others Do It

Franchisees of International Dairy Queen have learned that the biggest reason hourly employees leave Dairy Queen is a lack of proper training. When employees do not know what is expected of them, they naturally get frustrated and then they quit.

The core of training at Church's chicken chain is the Master Merchant program, which trains hourly employees in all aspects of the operation. A Master Merchant display board, which lists the names of all employees, is divided into three sections — cooking, serving, and process/cutting. When an individual becomes skilled in one area, which involves passing a performance test, a one-on-one verbal quiz, and a written exam, the job slot is checked off. When all three slots are checked off, that person becomes a "team leader" with responsibility for orientation and training for new employees. A modest pay increase is then awarded. There are other forms of recognition. For example, a saw pin is given for achievement in the cutting room. A special badge is awarded to the team leader who has mastered all three stations.

The Jolly Roger Company in California selectively screens employment candidates and then gives them intensive training. The manager selects two employees with outstanding skills to be training servers. They receive a twenty-five-cents-per-hour pay increase and take over the responsibility of teaching the operation to new employees. Each new employee is tested by the training server and by the manager, first at the end of the orientation period and then again after thirty days to maintain the standards.

At Pizza Inn in Dallas, training programs are conducted for waiters and waitresses as well as for managers. The goal is to foster one-on-one communications between the manager and each member of the service team.

Kentucky Fried Chicken has made a multimillion-dollar commitment to training. And has that investment paid off! The management from Heublein looks at training as an investment; the former management team viewed it as an expense. Because of training, turnover has been satisfactorily reduced; standards of quality, service, and cleanliness, as evaluated by mystery shoppers, are highly favorable; and fiscal 1980 operating profits were nearly double those of 1978.

For Heublein, the solution to problems of quality and service was to go back to the basics. A national training center was developed and staffed, and a training system for hourly employees called STAR (Star Training And Rating) was created. The overall program costs approximately $1.5 million a year.

There are ninety-nine lessons grouped into three major categories: general, food preparation, and customer service. The program is accompanied by audiovisual teaching aids and instructional manuals. Each employee's progress is charted on a STAR chart. When an individual completes a lesson, the manager records this fact on the chart next to the person's name. When all the lessons in a given category are fulfilled, a special STAR pin is awarded.

Mystery shoppers evaluate stores every month using forty different criteria, including product temperature, promptness and courtesy of service, and cleanliness. A perfect score is 100; a score of 90 is considered good. Over a two-year period, the scores of mystery shoppers' visits went from the 70s to the 90s. This was accompanied by reduced management turnover and increases in sales. As a learning and teaching tool, STAR has proven to be highly effective. It complements, but does not replace, a dedicated manager.

For an example from the hotel industry, let us see what we can learn from the experience of the Houston Oaks Hotel. After the initial interview and orientation sessions, new employees are thoroughly trained before they are put to work at their particular station. Once on the job, they are given periodic refresher training to maintain their high standards.

For example, there is a ten-session workshop for the room attendants. Early-morning classes are held twice a week for five weeks, with sessions covering policies, benefits, and rules; facts about the hotel and the chain; information on cleaning products; housekeeping terminology; staff organization; checking in, picking up key, picking up supplies, cleaning hallway, checking work cart (slide presentation); how to clean a bathroom, make a bed, put on a pillowcase, dust, place items in guest room; emptying linen and trash sacks, stocking cart, cleaning linen closet, making evening report, bringing down cleaning supplies, signing out; and the care of equipment and hotel security. The final session is a test.

❑ Training for Managers

Employees who are being prepared for positions as managers or supervisors are usually given the same training as other employees — and then some. For instance, the Jolly Roger restaurant chain spends more than $5,000 on each trainee before that person is ready to go to work. In eighty hours of classroom instruction, trainees learn people management skills through role playing and other group experimental techniques.

To assure uniformity in the communication and maintenance of service values and to avoid any possible erosion in standards, the companies in the Citicorp study provide their managers with intensive training sessions. Each individual can plan on going back to school at least one week a year for training in such areas as selection interviewing for job-related behaviors, employee orientation, group dynamics and how to run a successful meeting, teaching and counseling, progress reviews and feedback, one-on-one encounters as developmental opportunities, rewards and recognition, performance planning, performance standards, performance appraisal and feedback, constructive discipline that motivates, negotiation skills, conflict management, stress management, and time management.

These workshops are mandatory. In order to achieve consistency in the treatment of employees and customers, managers and supervisors must be trained. They must be provided with the skills to enable them to do this before they can be held accountable for results. The idea is that management can be learned, but it must be taught.

The purpose of these workshops is to provide managers and supervisors with the skills to enable them to lead and motivate well-trained employees, who will in turn be motivated to please the customer. An important part of the program is personal enrichment training. I have discovered that to achieve service excellence, personal enrichment training is usually more effective than trying to teach people to have a good attitude. (For more on workshop content, see Appendix G.)

I strongly advocate having the chairman and the president be visibly involved in the training sessions. Having them serve as behavioral role models is very effective in putting the training into practice. This is where it all begins — with total support and commitment. If other managers, supervisors, and employees observe the CEO's participation, the behaviors will stick.

McDonald's has a four-day management training program called "Managing the McDonald's Team." It has become a vital part of the curriculum of Hamburger University. Some of the topics covered in the four days include learning the manager's function, learning to set priorities, improving communications, motivating people, improving listening awareness, conducting performance reviews, recruiting and selecting crew members, recognizing signs of trouble, and developing your own store plan. Most of the learning is accomplished by role playing, simulation scenarios, and other participatory exercises.

At McDonald's, the best store managers and supervisors are selected to be full-time faculty members at Hamburger University. Teaching and training are judged to be too important to be left in the hands of the personnel department.

❑ **Evaluating the Training Program**

How does an organization know if its training efforts are effective? How does a company determine whether the training produces the intended result — fully satisfied customers and repeat business? These firms should always ask themselves, "After training, what will have changed and how will we know it has changed? When will the changes take place and what new skills will people have?"

It is simply not enough to have one good shot of training and then leave the results to chance. This is particularly true if somewhere along the line there has been some slippage in service superiority. A follow-up workshop serves to remind everyone of an organization's commitment to service.

In auditing the effectiveness of service training for consistency, management should use this approach: if sales and productivity figures are inconsistent, the likelihood is that the quality of the product or service is also inconsistent. A good overall philosophy is to give people responsibility and help and not bounce them for mistakes. Companies like to protect their expensive investment. Effective evaluations of training programs should address these questions:

- Which parts of the training were most effective and why?
- Which parts of the training were least effective and why?
- What was actually learned and retained?
- What was not learned or retained?
- How did the training help the individual do his or her job more effectively?
- Did customer satisfaction improve and to what degree?
- What are the major problems now being experienced in relating to customers?
- What difficulties or obstructions were encountered in ap-

plying what was learned? Why? What can be done to prevent these problems in the future?

- Which parts of the training should have been expanded or deleted?
- What else should be included?

To come up with this type of thorough evaluation, several questions must be asked and answered. What are the needs — real and imagined — of the participants and of the customers? How can we translate both sets of needs into measurable training objectives? What evaluation techniques will we use to measure our training objectives? How can we design the class to meet these objectives? After the training program, we must analyze the data, report it, and follow up.

❑ If You Can't Measure It, Walk Away from It

Any evaluation system should permit specific, quantitative measures. For example, the McDonald's management skills measurement system established measurable results. Store management turnover decreased 30 percent in the first half of 1980 compared to the year before. Communications between area supervisors and store managers improved, and this improvement was reflected in a management climate survey. Knowledge of various store management situations and measures of effectiveness increased 8 percent and 13 percent, respectively. General improvements in the management of store operations were clearly evident. The number of transfers among stores dropped 47 percent in the first quarter of 1980 compared to the first quarter of 1979. As the downward trend continued and was reflected in reduced turnover, first-quarter savings of over $100,000 were realized in a particular region. This included the average cost of recruiting, selecting, hiring and training. The program participants gave an overwhelming vote of confidence to the "Managing the McDonald's Team" training program and strongly recommended continuing and expanding the program.

APPRAISING CUSTOMER SERVICE PERFORMANCE

❑ *Identifying Problems and Finding Solutions*

Achieving a superior level of customer service, producing the kind of repeat business on which business success depends, is not a one-shot event. It demands a day-by-day, minute-by-minute dedication to preserving high standards. And that calls for a systems approach. In order to do this, it is necessary periodically to measure the gap between what is and what ought to be, and to correct any slips that show up.

The systems approach to customer service superiority is, in brief: first train to the exacting standards as defined, then continually audit performance against those standards to identify any possible slippage. During the course of the audit, it is important to examine these issues:

- What caused poor performance — inadequate experience, inability, unwillingness, understaffing, or ineffective supervision?
- How frequently does the problem occur? How much has it grown? How important is it to the customer?
- Has the problem been contained or does it continue to grow in size? What can be done about it?

- Who is affected by the problem in addition to the customers?
- What will happen if it is not corrected?
- What will it cost to solve it? How soon can we correct it permanently?

❏ Performance Appraisals

The next step is to take these evaluations down to the individual level. Frequent individual progress and performance reviews are vital to customer service superiority. If you have done your homework in establishing service standards and measurements, the individual employee should really know in advance of the review just exactly how closely his or her performance matches the standards.

Here, in outline form, are the ingredients of an effective performance appraisal system, what it should accomplish, and how to go about doing it.

I. What should a performance appraisal accomplish?
   A. Measure and evaluate the individual's contribution to business results.
   B. Do away with or at least reduce nepotism.
   C. Improve performance.
   D. Identify individual's strengths and weaknesses.
   E. Help to identify the better people and make them available for promotional opportunities.
   F. Bridge a communication gap between the manager and subordinates.
   G. Provide specific guidance and training opportunities for professional growth and development.
   H. Help a manager to evaluate his or her performance as a manager.

I. Recognize and show appreciation for good work.

J. Stress accomplishment as opposed to personality.

K. Look to future priorities and performance standards.

L. Result in specific, mutually agreeable goals for the next business cycle.

M. Relate performance to the reward system.

II. The objectives of the performance review

A. To evaluate the performance and potential of individuals regularly.

B. To assist the individual in building on existing strengths, overcoming weaknesses, and improving overall performance.

C. To assist the individual and the company in achieving superior operating results.

D. To assist the company in meeting its needs for managers by identifying potential talent throughout the entire company.

E. To provide a fair and equitable system of compensation that rewards excellent performance.

III. The problem-solving approach

A. Set up a positive climate for the upcoming meeting.

1. Ensure that the subordinate understands the purpose of the review session.

2. Emphasize the role your subordinate is expected to play as an active participant.

3. Ask the subordinate to prepare for the interview.

B. Prepare individually. (Both manager and subordinates should follow the same preparation steps.)

1. Review the subordinate's primary job responsibility — what is the person expected to do and what are the basic requirements?

2. Review the subordinate's key performance objectives.

3. Review the personal qualities, knowledge, skills, and attitudes needed.
4. Prepare a tentative evaluation.
5. Identify possible causes of less-than-expected performance and develop ideas for ways to achieve improvements.
6. Secure the next higher level of approval.

C. Conduct the interview.
1. Start the session.
   a. Put the subordinate at ease.
   b. Set a constructive tone for the interview.
   c. Clearly state the objectives of the session.
2. Evaluate present performance.
   a. Listen to subordinate's self-appraisal.
   b. Prepare an evaluation of the subordinate's present job performance.
   c. Discuss areas of difference about present performance, and work toward reaching agreement.
3. Analyze the causes of inadequate present performance.
   a. The subordinate's confusion about what was expected.
   b. The subordinate's unawareness of performance problems.
   c. The subordinate's lack of certain skills necessary for effective job performance.
   d. The subordinate's lack of motivation.
   e. Uncontrollable factors that affect the subordinate's performance.
4. Prepare for the future.
   a. Develop plans to improve performance.
   b. Identify specific action steps.
5. Conclude the session.

       a. Confirm agreements.
       b. Make feelings known.
       c. Decide whether another meeting is needed.
    D. Follow up on the performance review meeting.
       1. Complete final documentation.
       2. Arrange for future development activities.
       3. Monitor progress against objectives.
       4. Give timely feedback.

Another way to think about the performance review process is presented graphically in Figure 2, which suggests some questions that will help a manager stay on target when planning and conducting the appraisal.

A good manager recognizes that the performance appraisal is a tense time, and accepts the responsibility for conducting the interview in a positive, constructive way. Sensitive managers may well want to appraise their own performance, and ask themselves these questions in retrospect.

- Did I have clear objectives?
- Was the purpose of the interview made clear to the interviewee?
- Did I make the interviewee feel comfortable?
- Did I avoid doing other things while conducting the interview?
- Were my introductory remarks well prepared?
- Did I try to develop a good atmosphere for the interview?
- How well was rapport established with the interviewee?
- How well did I overcome any defensive attitude on the part of the interviewee?
- Did I talk on the interviewee's level in familiar terms?
- Did I instill confidence?
- Did I listen carefully?

FIGURE 2. PERFORMANCE REVIEW GUIDELINES

Performance Review   *Developmental Planning*

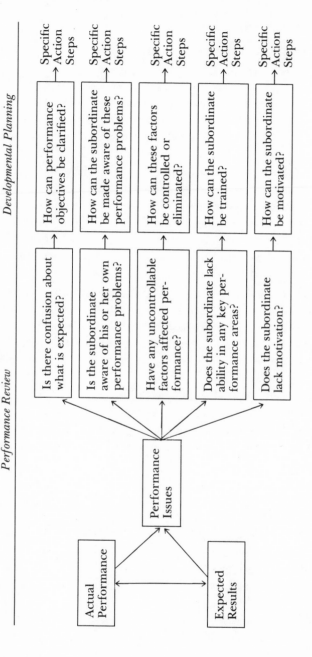

- Did I make an attempt to understand the interviewee's viewpoint?
- Did I avoid interrupting?
- Did I avoid snap judgments?
- Was I primarily nonjudgmental in my attitude?
- Did I work at attempting to see a point of view other than my own?
- Did I look for hidden indications of how the interview was going?
- Did I give the interviewee the opportunity to express feelings and emotions?
- Was I objective?
- Was I interested in what the interviewee was telling me?
- Was I encouraging to the interviewee?
- Did I use the technique of reflecting the interviewee's views and feelings?
- Did I avoid asking closed and dead-end questions?
- Did I summarize what had been said and decided?
- Did I give the other person an opportunity to ask questions?
- Was I repetitious?
- Did I give the interviewee the opportunity to formulate his or her own plans?
- Did I give unwarranted assurances?
- Did I try to get the interviewee to recognize his or her own problems?

❏ Performance Coaching

Closely allied to performance appraisal is the one-on-one technique I call performance coaching. It is an essential part of the total evaluation process and the systems approach to service superiority. It serves to maintain consistency in service over time.

Each of us views our job as advancing our own ends in the business world and becoming as successful as possible. And rightly so. But our success depends very largely and directly on our ability to make the people we manage as productive and successful as possible.

One of the most effective tools in accomplishing this is performance coaching. Performance coaching is a management tool to help managers identify and correct the real causes of nonperformance.

Think It Through

For this purpose, a one-on-one performance interview must be set up for reviewing unsatisfactory performance with the employee. Hold the discussion in a private place where it will not be overheard; make sure no one else is present and that no interruptions will occur. Get away from the office or work area, with all its distractions; avoid holding the discussion in a car where either of you is at the wheel. Allow plenty of time for the discussion.

Do your homework on the unsatisfactory performance in question, and make sure you are not making vague or general accusations. For example, if the problem is the employee's failure to handle difficult customers, have information at hand with specific incidents: who did what and how each reacted — the employee and the customer. Decide three things in advance: (1) what minimum action is acceptable as the outcome of the discussion; (2) what possible alternative solutions there may be; and (3) what the timetable for performance improvement is.

The First Step

To improve an employee's behavior, it is necessary first to identify what the employee is doing that is unsatisfactory. In an extraordinary number of cases, employees either do not know that their performance is not satisfactory or they simply do not know what is supposed to be done or how to do it. It is the task of the manager to clarify any of these points for the employee so that corrective action can be taken.

The first part of the performance discussion is the most critical and may take half the total time. Here, your job is to get agreement from the employee that a problem exists. This may not be as simple as it sounds, because many employees feel that their lack of performance in certain areas is no better or no worse than that of people around them. "Everybody else is late. Why are you picking on me?" Or they cannot comprehend that what they are doing constitutes a problem. "Oh, I didn't realize that I was being defensive or argumentative with the customers."

The best way to convince an employee that a problem exists is to make clear the consequences of unsatisfactory performance on several levels: to the customer, to the company, to fellow employees, or to the employee personally. For example, you could say, "By arguing with that customer, you aggravated the situation and upset others within earshot." Or, "When you're absent from your work station a number of times during the day someone else has to double up to cover your absence." If employees do not see their actions as a problem, they can hardly appreciate the consequences to themselves of what they are doing or failing to do. "I can't advance your name for promotion unless you improve your attendance to a satisfactory level." Or, "How can I give you an outstanding rating at the front counter unless the customer is satisfied?" The key here is to have the employee say, in these or similar words, "Yes, I agree that is a problem." Only then can you move ahead.

Discuss a Variety of Possible Solutions

Next comes a mutual discussion of solutions. Where there are alternatives available, it is important not to rank solutions or choose the most desirable, but simply to brainstorm all possible solutions that you and the employee can think of. Even the solutions that sound least likely can often trigger an idea from the other person. Remember, too, that this is a mutual process, where both of you must contribute. If the employee cannot contribute, then you must provide the necessary solutions. But as much as possible, allow the employee to suggest the remedies to be taken.

In many cases, employees do change and implement positive solutions to performance problems. But if you as a manager do not reinforce the employees' actions, they can easily slip back into their previous bad habits. If your employees continue to fail to improve their performance, you must know about it and offer them your continuing help. This may consist of going back to the list of alternatives and mutually choosing some new solutions if the previous ones did not work. Or it may mean clearing from their path some obstacles to the achievement of these solutions. "Why don't we role play and you be the disgruntled customer?"

Perhaps you must offer the employees further clarification of what you expect them to do, when it must be done, and how you will both know when it is done; for example, when a customer apologizes for being rude, it is clear that the employee remained calm and helpful throughout the discussion. To make sure you and the employees are on the same wavelength, ask them to summarize their understanding of the discussion. This lets you end the coaching session on a note of mutual agreement.

Obtain Agreement on Implementing Solutions

The next step is to arrive at a mutual agreement on which step will be implemented. "Okay, I'll start by catching the earlier train, and then walk from the station to work so I don't have to depend on the bus." Or, "I'll only make personal calls on my coffee break." The problem employee may want to settle for a general solution — "Okay, I'll do better." But you are after specific solutions, resulting in specific improvements that you can both agree on and measure. "I agree to be at work every day unless it is absolutely impossible for me to do so." Or, "I will make sure no customer leaves without a satisfactory solution to the problem."

Follow Up to Prevent Slippage

The fourth step is yours. You must follow up to make sure that the solutions you and the employee agreed on are implemented. If this step is not taken, all your work will have been wasted. Do not assume your employee will make the changes; make sure you audit him and measure him. You may encounter some resistance on this point from the employee. "Don't you trust me?" "I wish you wouldn't always watch me." "Either let me do my work in peace or take it away from me!" But remember, your job as a manager is to make sure that your employees are performing their jobs successfully. Explain to them that if you did not do your job and follow up their performance, you would be remiss on your own behalf as well as on theirs.

Recognize and Compliment Achievement

The last step is one of the most important in performance coaching. You must recognize any achievement when it happens. Do not wait for perfection, or even 75 percent improvement. When an employee demonstrates a noticeable improvement, your recognition can let her know she is on the right track toward solving the problem completely. Recognize any achievement and reinforce it as soon as possible after it happens. Thank the employee face to face today. And keep on providing recognition as long as improvement continues.

One more thing. If you promised a certain reward for improvement, come through with it. And do not keep promising the same reward for improvement in different areas. Find a different incentive for different solutions. "Since you have proven your abilities to deal with an angry customer, I'm recommending you for a pay increase."

Following the five performance coaching steps — getting agreement that a problem exists, mutually discussing alternative solutions, mutually agreeing on remedies to be taken, following up and measuring results, and recognizing any achievement promptly — will ensure your own success as a manager by helping your employees be as successful as possible.

❏ Evaluating the Manager

If there is one constant theme in the maintenance of service superiority, it is the behind-the-scenes motivation to foster positive service attitudes. Managers help employees develop these attitudes by thorough training, constructive appraisals, and effective corrective coaching. Let us not forget that the managers themselves receive their share of training, evaluation, and retraining. I still recall the McDonald's profit walkthroughs. Those very high standards of service superiority would never be compromised to achieve short-term profits.

The performance appraisals of the store management team reflected this philosophy. It was the underlying value of all the aspects of the manager's performance review, which included the following service components:

product freshness
holding times
product rotation
production calling
product sampling
condition of the equipment
attitudes toward customers
following closely the opening and closing procedures
crew development
communications
human relations
crew orientation
crew training
crew meetings
checks for calibration
service times
making time for the customer
helpfulness to the customer
no long lines
shift preparation
managing customer complaints
service support procedures
outside appearance of building and grounds
inside cleanliness
cleanliness at each work station
sanitation procedures
full staffing, crew and management
performance appraisals and wage reviews on time
affirmative action
crew incentives
crew enthusiasm

crew morale
crew activities

On all these items, and many others, each member of the management team was rated as above standard, standard, or below standard. If the majority of the ratings were not above standard, it was time to retrain.

In addition, McDonald's has an informal review process for managers called communication days, when they meet with area supervisors for a time of idea sharing and performance improvement. It is a blend of evaluation and training, and thus it exemplifies the total systems approach that typifies the companies that lead their industries in service superiority.

Each month, in each restaurant, one day is reserved for the area supervisor to spend time individually with each of the four or five members of the restaurant management team. The managers and assistant managers have the opportunity to discuss with the area supervisor their progress, their personal and professional goals, training, advancement opportunities, overall future with the company, and anything else that is on their minds.

The single biggest advantage, in my observation, is the rapport built between the area supervisors and their management teams. Communication days are opportunities to change behavior, to discuss and resolve special problems, to answer questions, to provide information and feedback, and to build on individual strengths while providing for the development needs.

This systems approach to service dedication can be found in any area, any industry. To emphasize the link between performance standards and performance appraisal, here is an example of a review spectrum for managers. It would be used to evaluate a supervisor who is responsible for management of five or six other supervisors of functional departments.

1. *Oral and Written Communications.* Defined as effectiveness in standup presentations, one-on-one encounters, conciseness and precision with words, keeping senior management informed, accurate and timely reports, and providing constructive input on policy issues and effective exchange of relevant information with other departments.

Excellent
- Demonstrates ability and interest in the need for policy change by frequently initiating and contributing to discussion of policy issues.
- Keeps senior management updated on all major problems and actions taken, whether internally or externally generated.

Good
- Passes information needed by other departments to those departments as requested; at times anticipates the need.
- Forgets to inform management of major changes; does not work effectively with other departments on occasion because of misinformation.

Below Standard
- Provides reports that are often late, incomplete, and difficult to read.

2. *Communications with Subordinate Managers.* Defined as demonstrated recognition of the importance of keeping team management informed of goals, direction, plans, progress, and information generally needed to improve operating efficiency.

Excellent
- Regularly distributes pertinent information in a timely manner to subordinate managers on all aspects that affect their operations.
- Keeps managers informed of any changes in policy, procedure, or direction.

Good • Ensures that managers pass on information from the supervisors' staff meeting.

• Does not listen well to subordinates; monopolizes the conversation and is too casual about the manner in which information is passed down.

Below Standard • Does not provide unit managers with necessary information concerning policies, procedures, and changes in direction.

3. *Training and Development.* Defined as demonstrated interest in and concern for the effectiveness of team training. In conjunction with unit management, decides on training requirements, priorities, progress, and recognition programs. Prepares unit managers for promotional opportunities.

Excellent • Delegates responsibility, accountability, and authority commensurate with the manager's abilities to accept same.

• Primarily supervises in a general sense, stressing operational effectiveness.

• Provides for profit walk-throughs along with audits of service quality and housekeeping on a regular basis with unit managers.

Good • Participates in unit manager meetings on a regular basis. Conducts oral and written examinations of trainee progress.

• Seldom has training meetings for assistance.

• Does not keep well informed of trainee progress.

Below Standard • Makes decisions for others and is not involved in training assistants.

4. *Problem-Solving.* Defined as the ability to recognize the real causes of problems as opposed to mere symptoms. Involves subordinates in problem-solving procedures. Implements creative solutions to problems so that they do not recur.

Excellent ■ Invariably involves unit managers in the problem-solving process. Can quickly identify and prevent potential problems from arising.
■ Offers timely solutions to problems when discussing them with upper management.

Good ■ Is good at solving short-term problems but is not adept at attaining longer-term solutions. Is averse to taking risks.
■ Can usually identify problems but procrastinates in solving them. Looks to others for solutions.

Below Standard ■ Allows small problems to become major problems because of inactions.

In a similar vein, evaluation standards are established for such areas as uniform and consistent application of company policies, relationships with managers in other departments above and below and social interaction with spouses, acceptance and fulfillment of administrative responsibilities, personnel relations with hourly paid employees, and personnel relations with subordinate unit managers.

The key point to be made here is that if standards are not used to measure the effectiveness of what happens within the organization or the individual function, systems will eventually break down. In the long run, only the customer will suffer.

MOTIVATING AND REWARDING CUSTOMER SERVICE EXCELLENCE

❏ *The Manager's Role*

The U.S. Chamber of Commerce and the Gallup Organization conducted an extensive poll involving a cross section of the United States in which they asked, "What changes would bring about the largest improvements in performance and productivity in most companies?" Over 80 percent of the respondents cited worker attitudes and abilities and managerial attitudes and abilities. A very small percentage noted that computerized facilities or more modern plants and equipment would make a significant difference. That same statement applies to the achievement and maintenance of customer service superiority.

Corporate America has drastically deluded itself on the impact of capital investment versus the potentially greater impact of investment in people. The real problem for business organizations — and for the millions of bored, underutilized, insufficiently challenged, and poorly rewarded employees — is poor management.

❑ Rewards and Recognition Are Built on Basics

In an article entitled "Building on Basics" for *Sky Magazine,* Mike Mescon discusses managers who make the right things happen most of the time. As his article points out, successful managers use motivation, training, communication, and recognition as their key management tools.

Lee Iacocca believes that things are even simpler; he says that the job of a manager requires but two basic talents: motivating and communicating.

Getting productive behavior from employees takes both reward and praise. Successful managers create and maintain winning teams by multiplying, strengthening, reinforcing, and rewarding exemplary behavior; by not being afraid to give thanks for a job well done. It takes a secure manager to praise and continue to praise.

In 1776 Adam Smith lauded the economy of high wages in his book *The Wealth of Nations.* He stated that productive behavior should be rewarded and not have a ceiling placed on it.

Seventy-five years ago, Frederick Taylor, often considered the father of scientific management, told us that the objective of management should be to secure maximum prosperity for the employer coupled with maximum prosperity for the employee. This pronouncement is equally valid today.

❑ Coach and Cheerleader

A good manager unleashes people power. Tom Peters, coauthor of *In Search of Excellence,* suggests that effective leaders orchestrate the band, wooing their employees, selling them dreams, and then helping them to realize and fulfill those dreams.

To be able to accomplish this, the manager must actually believe in the dignity and worth of every human being. The manager who trusts employees is self-confident and secure enough that employees do not merely perform jobs, they help to create and define them.

A senior manager at Procter & Gamble once told me, "The best manager is a cheerleader as well as a coach." And he lives up to his own standards. He works the second shift at least once a week, believing that those employees are also members of the team and deserve the same amount of coaching and cheering as the first shift.

The manager is the key to creating the kind of positive environment that encourages people to produce. This is particularly true in the restaurant industry, as was brought out in a review of several fast food chains. No matter which emphasis was chosen to improve productivity and customer service, certain attitudes were common to all the successes in the chains that were studied: having good communications between managers and service personnel, making each employee feel involved in the unit, and training both management and employees to do their jobs.

Stan Davis and William Wasmuth presented evidence in an article for *Cornell University H.R.A. Quarterly* that each incidence of employee turnover costs an average of $2,500. They point out that turnover costs could be reduced measurably without large expenditures by improving job satisfaction. Good managerial practices, effective supervision, and sensitivity to individual aspirations are all inexpensive to adjust, and they can greatly improve employee morale and hence productivity and service.

They also noted that in hotels, the food and beverage departments usually have one of the highest turnover rates —

more than 80 percent annually. We all know that high turn-over can kill our standards of service superiority. The poor quality of supervision was the culprit, according to 76 percent of managers who participated in the study.

George Odiorne, a leading management authority and author of the *George Odiorne Newsletter,* tells us that a great deal of attention has been paid to management style but too little attention has been paid to building trust. If employees can rely on their bosses to behave in a consistent and predictable manner, they can and will modify their own behavior to be more consistent, particularly in their relationships with customers and each other. And that is what creating and perpetuating service superiority is about. It is built on a relationship of mutual trust and openness between management and employees.

Let me tell you about a manager who is a shining example of this attitude, the supervisor of a midwestern dairy. He has a glass office in the middle of the dairy plant. He is available to all, and people stop in to see him when they have job-related problems. He helps them solve those problems. His role is clearly one of a coach who builds a winning team.

Once a week he takes a small group of employees out for breakfast, a different group each time. He buys that breakfast out of his own pocket. One of the questions he periodically poses is, "What can we do to help you to do a better job and how can we make this dairy a better place to work?"

This particular superintendent considers himself an enabler. He enables his people to achieve their fullest potential by removing obstacles in the pathway to success.

This dairy is healthy and profitable. It has put in a profit-sharing program to share the results of the company's success with those who contributed to that success. And best of all, there are virtually no service problems: no returns, allowances, shortages, or customer complaints.

Trust is built into an organization through the honesty and consistency of its management teams. For example, if some promises to employees cannot be kept, the employees are owed a thorough explanation. Similarly, if a budgetary allocation for additional staffing to provide better service must be trimmed, detailed reasons should be given to employees. That is the way to maintain the right attitude toward service.

Another key area for successful managers is building and maintaining high morale. Managers are usually loaded down with manuals of procedures and outlines of special employee programs. But the finest manuals in the world are a poor substitute for a manager's own enthusiasm. A supervisor's enthusiasm is a healthy form of contagion; other people catch it.

One of the most powerful motivating tools available to managers is positive reinforcement. Yet few managers practice reinforcement spontaneously. It is either nonexistent or negative. Never having received it themselves, they find it difficult to give.

An example of this power is the experience of Blue Cross and Blue Shield of Alabama. Four union-organizing drives over a five-year period gave evidence of a high level of employee dissatisfaction. This is anathema in a service organization — poor morale translates directly into poor customer service. This highly unsatisfactory situation was cured through a performance management system. Once performance management is solidly entrenched among managers and supervisors, it is brought down to the line-employee level in the form of performance teams. Performance teams focus on getting team members to reinforce positive behavior toward each other and toward customers.

First, sufficient data were collected to start monitoring employee performance and improvement in tasks. Then the technique of immediate and frequent feedback to employees was used. Last, managers and supervisors appropriately recognized and complimented employees for their performance improvement. Recognition comes in the form of verbal praise, encouraging notes, and minor cash awards.

In conspicuous places throughout the offices are signs that say "Find somebody doing something good and tell them about it." Managers now personally hand out individual performance reports to their employees. They give recognition and encouragement for additional improvement on a weekly basis. In the process they get to know their people better and help them by spending more time in solving performance problems. Employees feel better about themselves, their work, their company, their bosses, and their company's customers.

Another point in the roles of managers and supervisors is how to use happenstance encounters to reinforce the pivotal role of the customer. These one-on-one interpersonal events are viewed as developmental opportunities to motivate employees. Motivated employees motivate customers to come back. Every meeting, however informal, is used by management as an opportunity to practice leadership skills and to express appreciation or recognition when it is warranted. If the employee is recognized and appreciated, so is the customer.

Lest you be tempted to think that employees do all the work and managers have it easy, take a look at a typical day's "communication log." We might call it

One Day in the Life of a Manager

- Give information to subordinates.
- Interpret department policies and instruction.
- Instruct on what and how to do work.
- Make assignments to subordinates.
- Check on assignments.

- Follow up on general work progress.
- Get information.
- Advise subordinates at their request.
- Correct subordinates' mistakes.
- Praise subordinates.
- Stimulate subordinates to continue or increase effort.
- Lead conference to get advice or sell a conclusion.
- Persuade someone not responsible to you.
- Negotiate with equals.
- Conciliate or mediate dispute.
- Engage in chitchat.
- Make speeches inside and outside the department.

❑ Rewards and Recognition

Michael LeBoeuf, author of *The Greatest Management Principle in the World,* tells us that we get more of the behavior that we reward. People in an organization will do those things that they perceive will provide them with the greatest benefits. The manager's role in motivating employees to superior performance can be helped by formal and informal company-wide recognition programs.

To the service leaders in the Citicorp study it was clear that people do or do not do things on a something-for-something basis. This clarity of thought resulted in restructuring the reward and recognition systems to provide incentives for service superiority. They used many different techniques: internal contests, all the way from the local level to national competition for an all-American team; employee-of-the-month and unit-of-the-month recognition; displaying letters of appreciation from grateful customers (accompanied by cash awards); and publishing in company publications stories of employees who demonstrated outstanding customer-oriented behavior.

What are some of the things these role model companies did to heighten awareness and motivate service performance? To begin with, they recognized that wages and salaries were not a sufficient stimulator. Because employees need more than money, these companies added a variety of recognition programs to reward outstanding customer service. Although the programs naturally differ from company to company, these are some typical features:

- Employee recognition programs run continuously and change periodically.
- Service incentive programs change each year.
- A frequent theme used in employee incentives is "quality of service."
- Local manager's bonus program is tied to the volume of complaints received.
- Supervisor-of-the-year competition is continuous.
- Complimentary letters from customers qualify employees for outstanding service awards programs, which include cash prizes, televisions, paid vacations, and extra time off.
- All complimentary letters are placed in the employee's personnel file as well as sent to the home and posted on bulletin boards.
- Special recognition is placed on employee's name badge for outstanding service performance.
- Employees who have excelled in service to customers have their names published in normal bulletins, house organs, and listed in the column called "Service Beyond the Call."
- Instant rewards are given for superior performance.
- Mystery customers designate outstanding service employees, and these employees receive $25 rewards.
- "Blind" shoppers reward superior service with tokens that are then converted into dollars.

Over the years I have observed a number of creative approaches to recognizing and rewarding service superiority. Some of the best ones are using company publications to celebrate employees' special events, such as promotions, new hires, birthdays, retirements, public service recognition, and so forth; issuing green stamps for exemplary service; arranging frequent, informal parties to say "Thank you for all you've done"; using newsletters, house organs, bulletin boards, and letters sent home to publicize service excellence; providing health club memberships for the family; providing third-party employee assistance programs; arranging arts and crafts competitions; allowing for flextime, glide time, variable days, and a compressed work week, and providing trips, jackets, shirts, certificates, and caps.

From the time job candidates walk in the door until they retire, they are made to feel valued. All these little ceremonies add up to one thing, a message to the employee: "You are important and we treat you with respect." If the employee feels important, the customer gets treated like a VIP.

MEASURING CUSTOMER SERVICE RESULTS

In his book *Quality Is Free,* Phillip Crosby notes that although it is not easy to measure service quality, it is necessary to do so. He goes on to cite studies that show that 85 percent of the paperwork produced by organizations contains at least one error. The cost of fixing these errors is at least 25 percent of the operating expenses for that function. To put it another way, one dollar out of every four is spent in correcting mistakes.

If service superiority is to be maintained, companies must have a clear, measurable picture of how their customers perceive them. One mistake can cost a major customer. Fortunately the so-called soft areas, such as employee relations and customer service, can now be quantified and directly related to an organization's economic prosperity. The primary vehicle for accomplishing this is the survey.

At least once annually the companies in the Citicorp study survey everyone who has a relationship with the organization, to ask, "How well are we doing?" Survey data are gathered from customers, employees, supervisors, managers, community, visitors, and internal clients. All survey participants are encouraged to "tell it like it is," and their individual anonymity and confidentiality are guaranteed, since the results are sent directly to an outside consultant and tabulated by a computer.

Surveys tell management what people at all levels of the organization perceive to be the real values of that organization. This is particularly important because employees behave in accordance with their perceptions of what is rewarded and what is not. For example, if the survey question were to say, "The best performers get the highest rewards" and more than 25 percent of the respondents said they definitely disagreed with this statement, management would have a serious problem.

Just as important as performing the survey is how the data are used. Surveys raise expectations; issues and concerns are brought into the open. Participants have a right to know the results, as well as how management plans to address survey findings.

Another excellent reason for periodically asking people their opinions is the underlying message that is conveyed. Management is in effect saying to the employee, "You are important to us and we respect you. We care about you and we will use your inputs to make this a better place to work."

❑ What Is a Survey and Why Have One?

A survey provides a quantitative snapshot of an organization's health at a given point in time. It is designed to obtain specific opinions on specific subjects from specific groups of people. A survey literally measures what people perceive to be the facts in a given situation. And they will act according to these perceptions.

Surveys are highly important to management because they

measure the percent of satisfaction and dissatisfaction with the organization's products and services. They measure how well or how poorly an organization is functioning internally, in terms of how the various departments and functions service each other. They measure employee satisfaction and dissatisfaction with management. For example, professionally prepared and customized survey data can predict whether or not there will be a union-organizing drive and who will win it.

Survey data can also predict management and employee turnover. Suppose a management climate survey reveals that 25 percent of the managers say they are not free to make decisions and take actions necessary to perform their jobs. How long do you suppose those 25 percent are going to stay around?

Perhaps most important of all, surveys can tell a company what its customers think. When McDonald's conducted surveys of customer satisfaction, it learned exactly how many would come back for repeat business and how many would choose to go elsewhere to eat.

Certainly businesses can get a feel for the degree of customer dissatisfaction through a review of complaint logs, returns and allowances, letters of complaint, phone calls, employee and management turnover, grievances, strikes, slowdowns, theft, and sabotage. But it is impossible to quantify precisely the degree of dissatisfaction or pinpoint the real issues and concerns without survey data.

❑ Getting Started

Businesses that have never performed surveys may have some questions about how and when to get started. The key questions to be decided are given below.

Should a Consultant Be Used?

My recommendation is that an outside consultant should be used, if for no other reason than to guarantee the participants' complete anonymity and confidentiality. I have noted in many organizations a high negative response rate to questions dealing with the degree of openness and trust in management. This lack of trust carries through to the survey data.

Doing everything in-house is certainly more economical. But this greatly increases the likelihood of data distortion. If there is any suspicion at all, people will not give honest answers. They will tell management what it wants to hear. For example, I know of a hospital that conducted an in-house survey of employee attitudes. The results were highly favorable. Two months later they experienced a union organizing drive.

A good system is to have a lock box visibly present. The consultant can explain the particular instrument, the how and the why and what will happen afterward. Employees complete the survey, drop it in the lock box, and the consultant is off to the airport with the box. Employees feel more comfortable and provide more honest answers to some very touchy questions.

How Frequently Should Surveys Be Done?

Under normal circumstances, once a year is usually recommended for each of the surveys. My personal preference is to do one each quarter. This gives a company four quarterly snapshots, four different perspectives of an organization's health at four separate times within a calendar year.

If survey results show high percentages of dissatisfaction and game plans to address survey findings are quickly set into motion, my recommendation is to survey that same population using that same instrument six months later. One year is too long to wait to find out what impact changing management practices have had on important issues and concerns.

Suppose you had one or more of these four conditions in the first quarter of your fiscal year: a large layoff, a union-organizing drive, a significant increase in the size of the work force, or an extremely unfavorable survey result. My rule of thumb for those conditions is to survey semiannually.

Should Employees Be Told the Results?

Absolutely! A survey of any nature will raise the expectations of the population surveyed. When employees, customers, supervisors, and managers give their inputs, it is with the clear expectation that management fully intends to respond positively, quickly, and thoroughly to the issues and concerns they raised.

If management is unwilling to commit itself to feeding back survey results to all participants, and to addressing survey findings as quickly as possible, it is better not to do the survey at all. Conducting a survey but failing to take action says to the employees, "We're only trying to be nice; we never really intended to use your ideas anyway." The sample charts in the Appendix indicate my preferred way of feeding back survey data. The first showing is in private with the chief executive officer and the chief operating officer. The overall results are explained in detail.

What to Do with the Results?

This is perhaps the most important question of all. Turning the survey data into an action plan that will address the problems revealed by the survey is the hingepin for the entire process.

Table 1 displays an action plan developed by the current training manager at Procter & Gamble.

□ A Word of Caution

Attitude and climate survey results should not be used to hold a manager's feet to the fire, to find an excuse for discharging someone, or to bully a person into behavioral change. A survey will lose all credibility with participants if the results are used to initiate personnel actions such as terminations.

My own preference is first to familiarize supervisors and managers with the implications of survey results and their potential impact on productivity, profitability, and service. We discuss the situation, not the individual. We seek ways to manage more effectively. Rewards are neither given nor withheld for first-time survey results.

When commitments are made and action plans put together, the annual follow-up survey then becomes a basis for possible actions. At this stage people may be held accountable for survey results, because they will have made certain commitments, been given certain management skills training, and had a full year to initiate corrective actions based on survey findings.

When seeking a standard for evaluating attitude survey data, you will find that the most useful norms are your own data. Compare the different departments with each other and with the overall norms for the organization. Then compare both against themselves through the annual follow-up survey.

In an article for *Personnel Administrator,* Paul and Cheryl Lees-Haley issue a word of caution about the dangers of re-

TABLE 1. SAMPLE ACTION PLAN

Issue	Action Plan	Timing	Responsibility
1. Compensation and benefits			
Need for more information	Publish explanations in employee publication	Quarterly	Personnel
Desire for recognition	Issue employee handbook	October implementation	Personnel
	Conduct service award ceremonies	Annually	Personnel
Need for competitiveness in compensation	Publish CAP reports more frequently	Quarterly	Benefits administration
	Conduct annual benefits surveys	Annually	Corporate benefits
2. Management-employee relations			
Review of process/results achieved at weekly staff meetings			
3. Supervisory Relations			
Need for better explanation for performance expectation/standards	Identify training packages ■ Performance appraisal ■ Coaching/counseling	September implementation	Personnel
4. Career development			
Poor new employee orientation	Develop orientation program ■ History of company ■ Policies/procedures ■ Supervisory skills	June–September implementation ■ September ■ September ■ September	Personnel/managers

No coaching for career growth	Identify training needs for improved job performance	Complete	Personnel
Poor training on the job		Ongoing implementation	Managers/personnel
5. Working conditions Inadequate space	Move some units out of Tower 1	September	R & D facilities
	Redesign Floors 2, 3, 4	September	Personnel/facilities
	Move employees	December	Personnel/facilities
6. Management and operating effectiveness Inadequate staffing levels	Identify needs in resource plan	Annually (March–May)	All departments
Better communications to increase productivity	Conduct state of the business speech	Twice annually	Vice president and general manager
	Issue newsletter	Monthly	Personnel
	Share departmental objectives and progress	January and June	Personnel/departmental managers
	Conduct staff meetings	Weekly	Departmental meetings
	Issue policy manuals	September	Finance/personnel
	Conduct (a) orientation and (b) training	(a) As needed (b) Quarterly	Personnel

Source: Adapted from G. D. Searle Consumer Products Division, a division of Procter & Gamble.

lying on normative data. They note that reliance on norms can cause us to miss the intent of the survey, which is communication.

❑ Which Surveys to Use

Now let us look at four types of surveys, in the order I recommend you use them.

The Management Climate Survey

A management climate survey measures what people perceive to be the real values of the corporation. It measures how people react to an organization's culture — its values, norms, traditions, social mores, and sacred cows.

People behave in accordance with what they believe to be true. It is these very standards of expected behavior that determine how decisions are made and how problems are solved within an organization. These perceptions of values affect the performance of the management team, the individual's motivation, and the total collective performance of the business unit.

A management climate survey may include from 25 to 100 questions or more. It can be customized to focus on certain aspects of an organization's internal relationships. For example, a series of questions can be developed to find out how well each of a company's departments or subsidiaries services each other's needs, in terms of quality, service, timeliness, cost, and overall responsiveness. Results from a sample management climate survey are included in Appendix F.

By and large, most management climate surveys attempt to measure most of the following categories:

- clarity of an organization's goals and overall direction, coupled with a clear, shared understanding by its managers and supervisors of the plan for achieving these goals
- effectiveness of the decision-making processes in terms of quality, timeliness, and implementation
- organizational integration, cooperation, vitality — as a company, is the organization dynamic, healthy, and growing?
- effectiveness of individual managers — how well do various managers use their subordinates and how well do they treat them?
- degree of openness and trust — are people encouraged to speak up and voice dissenting opinions, or is a premium placed on not making waves?
- job satisfaction — to what degree do employees enjoy their work, pay, benefits?
- opportunities for individual growth and development — is there a chance to learn new skills to develop the talents and potentials of individual employees?
- performance orientation and accountability — are expectations and performance standards clearly spelled out? Does the system really reward results achieved?
- team effectiveness and problem-solving — are work goals for the department or the work unit clear to all and shared by all?
- overall confidence in management — are the employees comfortable with the way the organization is being run?

In order to determine just what the management style of a company is, the management climate survey is designed to measure both the effectiveness of individual managers and the overall leadership effectiveness. Anonymity and confidentiality are guaranteed because the survey results are mailed directly to the outside consultant and feedback is reported in cohesive work units of no less than five to ten people.

Here are some representative questions that deal with the effectiveness of individual managers. Survey participants are asked to give their honest and frank opinions by selecting one of five choices in response to each question: definitely agree, inclined to agree, undecided/don't know, inclined to disagree, or definitely disagree.

The person to whom I report . . .

1. thoroughly understands my job.
2. deals fairly and objectively with everyone.
3. periodically lets me know how well I am doing.
4. is relatively easy to see when I have a problem.
5. goes out of his or her way to solve problems with tact and diplomacy.
6. gives me all the information I need to do a good job.
7. respects me as an individual.
8. listens patiently to what I have to say.
9. encourages suggestions and input from me.
10. coaches me in my personal development.
11. appraises my performance fairly.
12. plans his or her work very well.
13. shares decisions affecting my work and my future with me.
14. supports me in my decisions.
15. actively encourages communication and cooperation with other departments.
16. encourages me to take reasonable risks.
17. provides positive feedback to me when I perform my job well.
18. communicates his or her expectations concerning my job performance.

You might find it enlightening to read some of the write-in comments that have been added to response sheets of some surveys I have recently been involved with.

"What business plan? Everything around here is a crisis, priorities are constantly changing."

"Will someone please tell me what I am responsible and accountable for? What are the performance standards for my job? On what basis am I being measured?"

"No one ever asks my opinion or tells me what's going on."

"When my manager asks for suggestions, he seldom uses them."

"The best performers don't get the biggest pay increases."

"How does my work relate to others in the organization? I don't know."

The Employee Opinion Survey

An employee opinion survey is designed to solicit feedback from employees at all levels of the organization concerning how they feel about their jobs, pay, benefits, working conditions, advancement opportunities, and recognition and respect received. This survey tells senior management how employees at every level feel about conditions that can both positively and negatively affect absenteeism, turnover, product and service quality, costs, and productivity. It also asks employees about the effectiveness of their bosses as managers. An employee opinion survey also measures people's feelings about organizational effectiveness, for example, cooperation and teamwork, goals and direction. And it measures the impact of the performance appraisal process and its ties to the reward system.

Results should be reported down through the first line of supervision and reviewed with each work unit. A plan to address and correct weaknesses and areas of concerns should be prepared, with responsibilities clearly assigned and target dates definitely established. A systematic, timely review of the progress made should be shared with all levels of management and all survey participants. A suggested format for an employee survey is included in Appendix B.

A special kind of employee survey is the exit interview, taken when employees leave the company, for whatever reason. If handled with sensitivity, the exit interview can provide companies with particularly useful information from an insider's perspective. The goal is to find out why employees are leaving an organization, because one must stop the flow of blood. We might think of the exit interview as a postmortem on management effectiveness. It can be done personally or by phone, but I believe it is better to do it personally. A sample exit interview, showing the main points that should be included, appears in Appendix C.

The Customer Satisfaction Survey

It is necessary to monitor customer service performance to let the organization know how effective its service policies, practices, and procedures are. A customer satisfaction survey tells the company where and how to take corrective action.

Many organizations already have available to them sources of information about customer satisfaction. The following kinds of systems should be monitored regularly, for they can provide much insight: complaint logs, product quality, service quality, billings, credits, accounts receivable, returns and allowances, delivery problems, letters from customers, suggestion systems, time lapsed between receipt of a complaint and corrective action, callbacks, sales representative and merchandiser feedback, service representative feedback, and direct solicitation for customer feedback.

The last point — direct solicitation — is of course where customer surveys come in. One characteristic of the service leaders in the Citicorp study is that they regularly seek out customer feedback, analyze it, and use the result in decision making, to close the loop on internal measurements.

There are numerous examples of survey formats capable of gathering this information from customers; you have probably encountered some yourself as a customer of hotels and airlines. Samples of such questionnaires are included in Appendix D.

When guests complete these surveys, hotel management should review the results very seriously. These surveys ask guests how well the promise was fulfilled by the delivery. To what degree did the organization perform according to its own exacting standards?

In the better hotels, anything less than a 95 percent favorable response calls for immediate action. An investigation is conducted. Standards are reviewed. More training is given if necessary. A hard look is taken at operational details to determine where and how slippage occurred. No stone is left unturned until things are made right and corrections taken to prevent a recurrence.

The Internal Client Survey

The internal client or internal customer survey is designed to measure how effectively the various departments within an organization respond to each other's needs and requirements. It quantifies people's perceptions of how effectively their business needs are being serviced within the organization. For example, a survey can measure the quality, timeliness, and responsiveness of the several departments or subsidiaries in terms of the products and services they provide for each other. A sample format is included in Appendix E.

The idea behind the internal client survey is that it is not possible to service customers properly if the organization does not have effective teamwork and cooperation among its various subsidiaries who supply each other with products or services. Excellence in customer service begins at home. Specific areas surveyed include the degree to which other departments

- fulfill your requirements for quality of service.
- jointly predetermine with you standards for quality of service.
- deliver service commitments in a timely manner.
- identify specifically who should be consulted to solve a service-related problem.
- understand your work, problems, obstacles, and requirements.
- take the initiative in identifying and solving service-related problems.
- are concerned with improving their own service effectiveness.
- plan their work to service your needs better.
- have clearly defined goals and standards for internal service.
- reward excellence in internal client service.

Following up on survey findings involves a similar process to following up on employee surveys and climate surveys — communicating results, establishing a game plan, setting specific responsibilities, and making provision for monitoring and recording progress.

LONG-TERM CUSTOMER SERVICE EXCELLENCE

❑ *Maintaining the Competitive Edge*

If the highest standards of service superiority are to be maintained in the marketplace, there must be no tolerance for mediocrity in any of an organization's operations, internal as well as external.

The best-managed organizations, including the seventeen companies in the Citicorp study, continually strive for perfection in everything they do. They know that once an organization achieves a superior level of customer service, it has no time to relax. Top-quality service needs to be sustained and reinforced, never allowed to slip; this is a continuing, never-ending process. All supervisors, all managers, and all employees at every level are continually reminded of the organization's customer-oriented values.

This process must reach every single employee, and it must start at the top. Management actions set the example. Employee awareness of the importance of customer service is influenced by the degree of importance management attaches to customer service, through its collective manifest behavior and the total budget it allocates to customer service.

❑ The Role of the Chief Executive Officer

The role of the chief executive officer (CEO) is to *personally* provide the overall service direction, actually write or endorse the organization's service policy, define the customer service objectives, and direct the overall integration of the organization's service efforts. Once the overall strategy and plans are formulated, the CEO provides the necessary funding, conducts quarterly service progress reviews, and evaluates service accomplishments against plans.

The CEOs of the successful companies in the Citicorp study for the most part were deeply and personally involved in the customer service function of their business. They personally read complaint logs and letters, took phone calls, and were highly visible and available to the rank and file. They both taught and attended training seminars and graduation banquets from in-house programs.

I can still recall how, in the early part of my career, the general manager of the Hotpoint Division of General Electric opened a training session with words of welcome and later passed out the certificates at the graduation banquet. Mostly I remember what he said: "If this were not important, I would not be here."

In a number of cases the CEOs of the role model companies participate in orientation sessions for newly hired managers to talk about customer-oriented values. They send constant signals throughout the organization that say, "We are and will continue to be a service-oriented company. We are in the business of service."

In *Quality Is Free,* Phillip Crosby points out that the credibility of the commitment is the biggest single problem for top management; it has to be reinforced all the time. He says that management has three basic tasks to perform: (1) establish the standards that employees are required to meet, (2) supply the wherewithal that employees need to meet those standards and requirements, and (3) spend time encouraging and helping those employees to meet those standards and requirements.

At McDonald's, top management strongly encourages everyone through its frequent visits to as many units as possible, both in the offices and in the field. During these visits, management talks with as many people as possible, stressing the importance of both the employee and the customer. At Levi Strauss, top executives frequently work as salespeople in the stores of their major accounts. They want to test consumer reaction firsthand. At McDonald's and Herman Miller there are no closed private offices; at McDonald's there are not even any doors! These practices are designed to encourage employees to take advantage of management's availability and willingness to listen.

In short, service leaders share an ongoing need to improve, a healthy sense of restless dissatisfaction with the status quo.

Preventing Service Problems

Crosby, in *Quality Without Tears,* tells us that anything that is caused can be prevented. Service problems are primarily caused by disenchanted employees, carelessness, lack of concern, poor training, imprecise service standards, lack of measurements, and poor follow-up. These things can be prevented. But prevention takes time and attention — top-management attention.

Crosby clearly places the responsibility for service superiority on top management's back. For example, he notes that if management does not provide clear performance standards, employees will develop their own. Too often management does not know, or denies, that it is the cause of the problem. Employees get turned off to the company and to its customers through the normal operating practices of their supervisors and managers.

Monitoring Service Measurements

But how does management know if the company has service-related problems? The simplest way to find out is through firsthand observation. Another way is continually and selectively to monitor and audit service policies, practices, and procedures. Still a third way is to ask — telephone, mail, survey, customer panels, focus groups, direct interviews, in-store surveys, mystery shoppers, even exit interviews of customers who do not come back.

There is yet one other way, particularly appropriate for the CEO: look at business results — the bottom line. Here is a checklist for the CEO to measure customer satisfaction, or the lack thereof:

1. Compare your market share with competition. Are you gaining? Losing? Holding your own?
2. Compare your sales growth against yourself and against the growth of the total market.
3. Compare yourself against yourself in terms of operating results and earnings as a percentage of sales.
4. Has turnover — of management, supervisors, and employees — decreased, increased, or remained the same?
5. Can you and do you measure the impact of service on return on investment? return on assets? earnings per share? new business? lost business?
6. What percent and how many dollars of your total budget are devoted to creating and maintaining service superiority, as contrasted with marketing and new sales?

Additionally, the CEO needs to pay close personal attention to the following:

- customer complaint logs, letters of complaint, and phone calls
- reports of mystery shoppers
- survey data on outside customers, employees, supervisors and managers, and inside customers
- programs for communicating, accepting, and enforcing precise service standards for both internal and external customers
- service goals and their degree of attainment
- service budgets
- productivity per employee
- sales per employee
- employment costs as a percent of total costs (are they increasing? decreasing? stable?)
- profit per employee
- costs of service complaints
- interval between the time a customer registers a complaint and the time it is satisfactorily settled
- grievances, strikes, sabotage, absenteeism, sitdowns, slowdowns, and walkouts
- whether the best performers receive the highest pay increases, and whether the margin of difference is significant
- performance appraisal reviews and discussions
- how customer service excellence is rewarded
- field service and field sales reports

Changing the Culture

If service-related problems continue to be a major source of concern, if survey results are disappointing at best and customers are slipping out the back door, never to return, a company may need to change its culture. Crosby notes that in order to stop hassling the customer forever, it may be necessary to change the company's culture, to eliminate the causes that produce nonconforming products or services.

Changing the culture is possible, but it does take time. Jan Carlson, president of Scandinavian Airlines, changed his company's culture to give primary emphasis to service superiority, including service quality, service timeliness, and service delivery. On-time flights became the rule. In two years, the airline moved from a loss to a handsome profit.

In order to change a company's culture, management must have three things: a recognition of the need to change, coupled with knowing what to change, based on appropriate diagnosis; the capacity and willingness to make the needed changes; and the skills and competencies to manage and implement the needed changes. The skills to manage the changes normally include a change in management style and direction; more demanding performance standards, including lessened tolerance for mediocrity at all levels of the organization; skills in total performance management, including precise goals, strategies, standards, appraisals, and feedback systems; more effective negotiation and communication skills; counseling and progressive discipline; and readiness to make difficult "people" decisions.

Setting a Higher Standard

To avoid slippage and the necessity for subsequent culture change, companies must continually test, refine, and improve their existing standards of service superiority. They must reward lavishly those who meet and then exceed their standards for quality of service. And once a standard is being consistently met, the CEO must set a new, tougher one.

The seventeen service role models never let up for a moment. They continually reinforced and rewarded the correct behaviors. It has been noted that they constantly developed and introduced new programs and new means to reward outstanding service to customers. They made liberal use of service audits to monitor service policies and practices. The ongoing, lifelong nature of training must be emphasized and then re-emphasized to achieve and maintain service superiority. The high level of expectations management sets for employees can be even more important than the actual training received.

❏ Maintaining Morale for Service Superiority

It is the CEO of an organization who sets the tone and overall commitment to customer service. But it is the rank and file employees who are out there on the front line, with the responsibility of carrying out that policy. A big question for all those in senior management is how to keep morale high among employees, especially during the time problems are being worked out. How does a company keep its service team committed when things go wrong? I can tell you firsthand how McDonald's does it.

McDonald's management recognized that everyone is not "up" all the time, so they came up with the personnel action manual. This was a people-oriented cookbook of ideas on how to keep the job interesting and motivating for the crew person.

The programs were designed to sustain enthusiasm but were not intended to substitute for basic good human relations practices. It was reiterated that solid, day-to-day human resources management is first and that this should be complemented by regular, positive, upbeat performance reviews.

Weekly informative meetings for employees were still as essential as ever, and above all so was the manager's own example of a pleasant demeanor, motivation, enthusiasm, and a service orientation. The basic idea behind all these action plans was to maintain a constant state of high enthusiasm. We will look at the specific ingredients in a minute. But first, I want to tell you a story.

John was a minimum-wage employee at a messenger service company. He was considered an ideal employee — cooperative, committed, honest, and enthusiastic. Then one day, for no apparent reason, John threw his delivery down the elevator shaft. He left the company without notice and did not even return to pick up his final check.

What happened to John can also happen in your organization. People do have problems — personal and professional. However, if the work environment continues to be warm, comfortable, and friendly, with something exciting in the air, people will actively look forward to coming to work and giving the best they can to each other and to the customer. They tend to forget their personal problems and immerse themselves in their work.

Now, some ideas you can borrow from McDonald's.

The Enthusiasm Calendar. The essence of an enthusiasm calendar is to select for each month an activity appropriate to the season and then to build on that idea and reward employees for successful participation. To make sure everybody at McDonald's understood the calendar, it was posted on the bulletin boards and discussed in a weekly informative meeting for employees.

For example, April is a great month for spring cleanup. Get everybody involved in how best to do this. Perhaps sometime during the business quarter you may wish to do a reverse performance appraisal, where the employees confidentially and anonymously evaluate and appraise the effectiveness of their bosses as supervisors. Any combination of ideas can be plugged into the enthusiasm calendar.

The All-American Team. Designed to upgrade quality, service, and speed, the all-American team is basically a healthy, head-on competition between units — for example, several branches or stores performing the same work. The underlying purpose is to establish management's criteria qualitatively and quantitatively and then to communicate these criteria. For example, typical criteria in a restaurant could include sales per person, delivery time, quality of service, accuracy of service, dependability of the crew, and versatility (since most people can work several stations with equal effectiveness).

The Communication Log Book. To be sure employees do not say, "I don't know" or "It's not my job," they must be kept informed of what is going on. A communication log can help achieve this objective. It is limited to very important messages from management. In addition to posting the message on the bulletin board, a memo is circulated to all office employees. Remember, one of the tenets of meticulous attention to detail is that nothing can be left to chance.

Costume Parties. On a special occasion such as Halloween, appoint a volunteer employee activities committee to plan a costume party. Give them a firm budget and have them arrange a party with refreshments. Hold the party in the office, but clean it up, spruce it up, and decorate it. Give a prize for the best costume and have the activities committee serve as the panel of judges. Sounds crazy, but it sure does seem to work at all levels of the organization.

Employee Involvement. This is similar to employee participation. Those involved in a special management project, such as decorating for a party, will be more committed to a goal. The committee should always include the better performers. The group should be changed frequently to make sure that people have an opportunity to rotate. The assignment should be kept short-lived and temporary.

There are all kinds of activities and projects that employee committees can be involved in: for example, a review of service performance standards, the appraisal system, safety, and community relations. Let their imaginations guide them, as long as they end up with specific suggestions to management. Management in turn should adapt and incorporate as many of these ideas as possible, in particular those dealing with service superiority and keeping the customer happy.

Informative Meetings for Employees. It is important to hold informative meetings frequently and to make them an interesting and pleasant experience for employees. For example, one meeting might begin by having the employees nominate the best employee of the week in a particular job category. Have them define their criteria, nominate three or four candidates, take a vote, and give a prize or an appropriate reward to the winner in front of the group. Or you might begin your informative meetings by offering special recognition, for example, to the top employee of the month or to those who have received a scholarship, made the honor roll, or celebrated birthdays. The essential thing is to vary the meetings and the tone to keep them interesting and lively as well as informational.

Employee of the Month. In industry in general and in retailing in particular, the excellent practice of recognizing the employee of the month has become fairly commonplace. Sometimes a variation in the theme can help to keep it lively. For example, management usually chooses the recipient in relation to predetermined criteria, such as the existing appraisal system or excellence in customer service. One variation would be to have the employees themselves nominate and vote for the employee who has achieved the highest standards of customer service. This is an excellent way to build employee awareness. Many companies have this regular practice, and it inevitably gets the best mileage from the crew.

Awards need not be expensive. As little as $10 to $15 is adequate. Be sure it is accompanied by publicity, using bulletin boards, letters to the home, plaques, special parking places, and so on.

I have seen the eyes of McDonald's crew members who were singled out as the employee of the month light up like pinball machines and stay that way for weeks thereafter, particularly when the award was given in the presence of the employee's peer group. It works with equal effectiveness among managers.

Using Employees to Set Service Goals. The management team sets goals for service improvement in conjunction with the crew. Employees will achieve higher standards of performance for themselves if they participate in the process of setting their own goals. The basic premise of quality circles, for example, is to let employees participate in decisions that affect them. They can help to decide what is most important and come up with realistic game plans to achieve those goals. Management, of course, does not abdicate its role.

The Employee Trainer. Take the exceptional employee and convert her into a part-time trainer. She then serves as a role model for other employees. Through her performance and the use of constructive criticism, patience, and enthusiasm, she quickly acquaints the new employee with excellence in customer service. This approach is more formalized and is preferred to the old "buddy system." On the one hand it helps to build quality, speed, and accuracy. And for a few cents an hour, say twenty-five to fifty cents, a load can be taken off the busy supervisor's back.

Job Rotation. Boredom is one of modern industry's greatest challenges. Bored people atrophy. Or quit. But people who are challenged to learn new skills, and then to master them, rightfully feel that they are growing. Those people tend to stay around.

One way to give people opportunity for growth is through rotating jobs. This has the additional benefit of giving an organization more flexibility and providing backups for highly skilled jobs.

McBingo. The idea of McBingo is simple but effective. Managers prepare some bingo cards with all the store stations included in separate boxes. For each box, the performance standard is clearly defined. As an employee meets that standard, the box is filled in. Five lines in any direction earn an award. When a person completes the entire card, he or she gets a raise. The contest usually lasts up to three months.

McBucks. A simple reward for achieving customer service goals, McBucks can be earned by employees who demonstrate excellence in customer service in some form, shape, or manner. Nominations may be made by the employees, but the actual rewards are the sole prerogative of management. Some of the criteria I would propose for the awards include cooperation and teamwork, volunteer help, going beyond the call of duty, dependability, number of employee referrals, and nomination by other employees. Play money or Monopoly money can be used; at the end of the month it is converted into real dollars.

The Number 1 Club. We simply cannot say enough about rewards and recognition. The whole purpose of the Number 1 Club is to provide special recognition for exemplary customer service. Required first are detailed, precise, quantitative performance standards, accompanied by a clearly communicated system. Once these are in place, eligibility requirements for the Number 1 Club are also defined. Some of those eligibility requirements could include, for example, length of service, performance appraisal ratings, examination scores, and peer review and input.

Refer a Friend. People who were referred for employment

by other employees generally seem to work out well. Give the employees an incentive to tell friends and neighbors about your organization, then reward them for the referral. The reward does not have to be expensive — a $10 reward costs a lot less than newspaper ads. It is also a good idea to tie part of that referral bonus into the retention of the new employee, say for a period of three months or more. Some companies tie part of that bonus back into the performance rating of the new employee.

Rookie of the Month. One of the most successful motivators I observed at McDonald's was Rookie of the Month and Rookie of the Year for each of the functional disciplines. The idea is simple, and it can be used monthly, quarterly, or annually. The individual may be nominated by management or fellow employees. The awarding of the certificate should be accompanied by the appropriate ceremony and congratulations from the entire management team in the presence of the peer group.

Employee Social Events. As an organization grows, expands, and hires more people, the feeling of closeness enjoyed in the earlier days is sometimes forgotten. The family atmosphere can erode to the point that employees feel no one cares about them. One proven method of avoiding this is the use of periodic social or sporting events. Many organizations do this, with great positive effect on morale.

The employee activity committee referred to earlier is solicited, the volunteers are given a budget, and they create the appropriate calendar of social events. During the year these could include such things as a family picnic, Christmas party, athletic team, bowling night, family day, open house. There is no limit to their imagination. Their enthusiasm quickly reflects itself in service at the customer level. This is one of the best and least expensive ways to create a service team. A social event builds commitment and team spirit.

Customer Awareness. Just as the advertising people strive to create top-of-the-mind product awareness, the organization must also create and maintain top-of-the-mind service awareness in all employees. Nothing is more important.

The best management example I can think of is the time that Ray Kroc got out of his chauffeur-driven limousine in a McDonald's parking lot, picked up a hamburger wrapper, went inside, and fired the store manager in front of the crew. He wanted to make an example of the fact that cleanliness and pleasant surroundings are an integral part of customer service.

Once slippage in service is noticed but not corrected, the slippage becomes a new standard. As an interesting sequel, the fired manager, a good worker, was rehired and transferred to another store. Whenever Kroc came back to town, we quietly gave him the day off.

This same concept can be applied, perhaps with a little more subtlety, through the white glove inspection. This can be done by a mystery shopper or a regular management employee from another area. It emphasizes that cleanliness is an important part of service. The mystery shopper runs a white glove in not easily visible places — for example, above the doorjamb in the restaurant. If the glove comes out dirty or greasy, the store receives an unfavorable write-up. If clean, it receives a citation.

❑ One Final Word

This book is all about customer service. Not adequate customer service, but exemplary customer service, service so superior that customers will not be motivated to take their business anywhere else. The principles can be applied to any business, from giant to neighborhood stores. To be sure you do not think this is about megasystems that can be implemented only by international firms with billion-dollar budgets, let me tell you a story about one of the most successful businesses I know. And one of the smallest.

There is a small dry cleaner in Skokie, Illinois. My wife drives fifteen minutes out of her way because the proprietor makes her feel like an old friend. Occasionally she gives Margo a small silk scarf. She carefully inspects each garment, making all the necessary repairs, replacing buttons — all at no extra charge. This delightful woman told my wife, "I know you do not live here. There are many places where you can take your cleaning, so I treat you special because I want you to come back."

And that, my friend, is what service superiority is all about.

Appendixes
References
Index

A JOB DESCRIPTION FOR A TRAINING DIRECTOR

I. *General Information*

Position Title: Training Director
Incumbent: Open
Department: Human Resources
Reports to:
Prepared by: Robert L. Desatnick
Approved by:

II. *Purpose of the Position*

The purpose of this position is to improve business and operating results through creation, design, implementation, and conduct of complete training systems for Services, Inc. Position will affect all levels of management, supervision, and employees.

Initially the incumbent will conduct needs analyses to determine greatest opportunities for productivity and profitability improvement. Those needs analyses will then be translated into concrete training programs with measurable objectives. Individual will train and certify trainers to carry on program.

III. *Position Responsibilities*

    A. Conduct training needs analyses to determine opportunities for productivity and profitability improvement in such areas as new employee orientation, job skills training, supervisory and management training for the following categories of people:

        1. Messengers, inside and out
        2. Customer service reps
        3. Supervisors/dispatchers
        4. Branch managers
        5. Clerical staff support
        6. Office supervisors
        7. Middle and upper management

    B. Design and prepare appropriate instructional materials such as manuals, videos, tapes, and train-the-trainer guides.

    C. Design, develop, and conduct training sessions in such areas as

        1. New employee orientation
        2. Job-related skills
        3. Telephone courtesy
        4. Customer relations
        5. Performance planning
        6. Performance coaching
        7. Progress reviews
        8. Motivation
        9. Performance management
      10. Effective staff and employee informative meetings
      11. Rewards and recognition
      12. Listening skills
      13. One-on-one communications
      14. Constructive discipline
      15. Managing a problem employee
      16. Managing a difficult customer

17. Negotiating skills
18. Conflict management
19. Stress management
20. Time management

D. Design and conduct train-the-trainer sessions for employees, supervisors, and managers to encompass part or all of the above as appropriate.

E. Design, develop and apply
   1. Training objectives for each course
   2. Measurement and evaluation of training effectiveness

F. Serve as training adviser and consultant to Services offices in other cities, such as Washington, Boston, Chicago, and Los Angeles.

G. Work closely with facilities manager to provide assistance if and as appropriate in his conduct of classes dealing with the Services selection system and the introductory management skills training.

H. Periodically report to management the quantitative and qualitative results of training in such areas as
   1. Employee and supervisory attitudes and motivation
   2. Gains in productivity
   3. Reductions in customer complaints
   4. Cost savings and operating effectiveness
   5. Improvements in attendance and retention

I. Keep abreast of the latest developments in training media, methods and devices such as interactive videos, training and instructional aids, measurements of training effectivess. Apply to Services as appropriate.

IV. *Educational, Experiential, and Skills and Abilities Preferred*
   A. *Educational:* Prefer a bachelor's degree in communications, liberal arts, and/or business administration.
   B. *Experiential:* Four to seven years progressively re-

sponsible experience with a fast-paced, dynamic organization which employs substantial numbers of hourly paid employees. Example: hotels, retailing, or fast foods

C. *Skills and Abilities Required:*
1. Analytical — job analysis
2. Sense of urgency
3. Internal consulting skills
4. Communications, oral and written
5. Judgment/decision making
6. Flexibility and adaptability
7. People development and training skills
8. Facilitative skills
9. Cooperation and teamwork
10. Ability to work under pressure
11. Problem solver
12. Listener
13. Self-starter — initiative and motivation
14. A team player, cooperative
15. Dependability
16. Professional standards
17. Ability to work effectively at all levels of the organization

A SAMPLE EMPLOYEE OPINION SURVEY

Your management asks you to fill in this questionnaire because they want to know how you feel about your job here. They want this information also as an aid to them in trying to run this operation more efficiently.

Notice that the questionnaire has several parts, and that there are specific instructions for each part. Please read these instructions carefully before writing your answers.

The statements in the questionnaire (that is, its "questions") have been constructed so that your response will reflect your attitudes and opinions. There are no right or wrong answers. The proper answer for you, therefore, is the one which best shows how you yourself feel about the matter.

Please answer *every* item. Don't skip any. If you are not sure of the meaning of any statement, please ask the person in charge of the survey to explain it to you.

Please do not discuss the statements with anyone until after the meeting. We want you to express your individual opinions without being influenced by your fellow employees.

This survey is only as useful to you and to your management as you make it. In other words, it can be valuable only if you express your attitudes honestly and frankly according to the way you yourself feel about each statement.

The answers are scored by machine according to each *group* of employees. No *person* can be identified in this survey. The questionnaires will be destroyed as soon as the scores for each group are completed.

Please record your attitude toward each statement by putting an X under the answer you choose. For example, please put an X under:

- *Definitely agree:* if the statement definitely expresses how you feel about the matter.
- *Inclined to agree:* if you are not definite, but think that this statement tends to express how you feel about the matter.
- *Inclined to disagree:* if you are not definite, but think that the statement does *not* tend to express how you feel about the matter.
- *Definitely disagree:* if the statement definitely does *not* express how you feel about the matter.

The statements in this part of the questionnaire express a wide range of feelings that a person might have about her job. In recording *your* feelings, please indicate what *you* think about *your* job — what you like about it, and what you dislike. You can do this by showing how much you agree or disagree with each statement.

In some of the following statements, the term "department" is used. This refers to the office or branch where you work. Your manager is the person to whom you report.

	Definitely agree	Inclined to agree	Inclined to disagree	Definitely disagree
1. I enjoy my work here.	—	—	—	—
2. I am satisfied with the salary I now receive.	—	—	—	—
3. Decorations and furnishings in my office are not in keeping with the kind of job I have.	—	—	—	—
4. I am satisfied with my chances to be promoted to a better position (higher level) in the future.	—	—	—	—
5. Too frequently I am kept in the dark about what goes on around here.	—	—	—	—
6. The people I work with always have the time to give the information I need to do my work.	—	—	—	—
7. I am satisfied with the extent to which the work I am now doing is receiving the recognition and respect of my associates.	—	—	—	—
8. I get a great deal of satisfaction out of my work because it means being connected with a successful (profitable, effective) operation.	—	—	—	—
9. I feel that my job is not classified at a sufficiently high position level.	—	—	—	—
10. We need more privacy in our office arrangement.	—	—	—	—
11. I am satisfied with my chances in the future to do work which offers good opportunities for continued growth in my profession or technical specialty.	—	—	—	—
12. My manager always lets me know beforehand of changes that affect my work.	—	—	—	—

	Definitely agree	Inclined to agree	Inclined to disagree	Definitely disagree
13. The people I work with often are too busy to help me when I need the service they are supposed to provide.	—	—	—	—
14. I am satisfied with the extent to which the work I am now doing will probably have a significant influence on the future of the company (or of my department).	—	—	—	—
15. I get a great deal of satisfaction out of my work because of the good products we make (or good services we render) in this department.	—	—	—	—

AN EXIT INTERVIEW QUESTIONNAIRE

To be completed for each terminating employee.

Name _____

Office _____

Job title _____

Date interviewed _____

By _____

Termination date _____

Supervisor _____

We want to make this organization a better place in which to work, and we need your help to do so. Would you please spare five or ten minutes of your time to answer a few questions?

1. If you accepted another job, what does that job offer that your job here did not?
2. What were the factors which contributed to your accepting a job with this company? Were these expectations realized? If not, why not? Has that changed in your present job?

3. Was the job you held accurately described when you were hired? To what extent do you feel that your skills were utilized?
4. What constructive comments whould you have for management with regard to making our organization a better place in which to work?
5. What are some of the factors which helped to make your employment enjoyable for those parts that you liked?
6. Would you recommend this company to a friend as a place to work? If yes, why? If no, why not?
7. Was your decision to leave influenced by any of the following? Please check all those that are applicable.

Leaving the city   —
Returning to school   —
Health reasons   —
Family circumstances   —
Retirement   —
Secured a better position   —
Dissatisfied with:
     type of work   —
     working conditions   —
     salary   —
     supervision   —
     other (please specify)_____

8. What did you think of the following in your job or your department? (please pick one)

	Excellent	Good	Fair	Poor
▪ Orientation to job	—	—	—	—
▪ Physical working conditions	—	—	—	—
▪ Equipment provided	—	—	—	—

	Excellent	*Good*	*Fair*	*Poor*
▪ Adequacy of training	—	—	—	—
▪ Fellow workers	—	—	—	—
▪ Cooperation within the department	—	—	—	—
▪ Workload	—	—	—	—

9. What was your attitude regarding your supervisor/manager?

	Excellent	*Good*	*Fair*	*Poor*
▪ Demonstrates fair and equal treatment	—	—	—	—
▪ Provides recognition on the job	—	—	—	—
▪ Resolves complaints and problems	—	—	—	—
▪ Follows consistent policies and practices	—	—	—	—
▪ Informs employees on matters that directly relate to their jobs	—	—	—	—
▪ Encourages feedback and welcomes suggestions	—	—	—	—
▪ Knowledgeable regarding performance and accomplishments of employees	—	—	—	—
▪ Expresses instructions clearly	—	—	—	—
▪ Develops cooperation	—	—	—	—

10. What is your opinion regarding the following? (choose one)

	Excellent	Good	Fair	Poor
▪ Your salary	—	—	—	—
▪ Opportunity for advancement	—	—	—	—
▪ Performance appraisal	—	—	—	—
▪ Company policies	—	—	—	—

(If fair or poor, tell why.)

EXAMPLES OF CUSTOMER OPINION SURVEYS

❑ Passenger Survey

Section One: Some Facts About This Flight

1. In which section are you traveling? *(circle one)*
   1 First class
   2 Coach
2. Who paid (or will pay) for this ticket? *(circle one)*
   1 Company, client, business associate, or government
   2 Yourself
   3 Relative or friend
3. The primary purpose of this trip is *(circle one)*
   1 business.
   2 personal.
4. Could you have made this trip on another airline? *(circle one)*
   1 Yes   *If so, why did you choose our airline?*
1 price	4 reputation
2 convenient time	5 frequent flyer program
3 quality of service	6 other _____
	(please specify)

   2 No

Section Two: Your Opinion About Our Service

5. Please rate the service you've received from us. *(circle one number for each area listed)*

	Out-stand-ing	Good	Ave.	Poor	Does Not Apply
a. When making reservations:					
efficiency of personnel	5	4	3	2	1
friendliness of personnel	5	4	3	2	1
b. At the airport:					
efficiency of personnel	5	4	3	2	1
friendliness of personnel	5	4	3	2	1
boarding process	5	4	3	2	1
baggage claim	5	4	3	2	1
on-time departure/arrival	5	4	3	2	1
c. On the airplane:					
efficiency of personnel	5	4	3	2	1
friendliness of personnel	5	4	3	2	1
cabin cleanliness/comfort	5	4	3	2	1
meal/beverage service	5	4	3	2	1
inflight magazine/audio selection	5	4	3	2	1

6. How would you describe our airline? *(circle only those that you feel apply)*

1 Reliable	5 Convenient
2 Efficient	6 Affordable
3 Friendly	7 Competent
4 Innovative	8 Responsive

7. How would you rate the value of your flight today based on its cost? *(circle one)*

5 Excellent	2 Poor
4 Good	1 Very poor
3 Average	

8. All things considered, what is your overall opinion of this flight? *(circle one)*

    5 Excellent   2 Poor
    4 Good   1 Very Poor
    3 Average

9. Compared to other airlines, our airline's . . . *(circle one for each)*

	Better	Same	Worse
overall service is	3	2	1
value for the money is	3	2	1

10. If all airlines had the same schedules and fares, which would be your first choice?

_____

(specify airline)

Section Three: Some Facts About Your Travel

11. About how many flights have you made in the last twelve months, including this one? *(count round trips as one flight)*
    _____ *(number)*

12. How many of these flights were primarily for business purposes?
    _____ *(number)*

13. And how many of these flights were made on our airline?
    _____ *(number)*

14a. Are you a member of any frequent flyer program, that is, a program that offers free trips for accumulating mileage?

    1 Yes   Please answer questions 14b, 14c, 14d, and 14e
    2 No   Please skip to question 15

14b. In which airline's mileage program do you most actively participate? *(circle two you most frequently use)*

1 American   6 PSA
2 Continental   7 Republic
3 Delta   8 TWA
4 Eastern   9 United
5 Frontier   10 Western

14c. Other than flight schedules and destinations, why did you join the frequent flyer program you use most often? *(circle all that apply)*

1 First class upgrades for joining
2 First class upgrades for a nominal charge over the full coach fare
3 First class upgrades on the reward chart
4 Reduced air fares
5 Free trips
6 Mileage bonus for joining
7 Hotel tie-ins
8 International airline tie-ins
9 Rental car tie-ins
10 Other _____
(please specify)

14d. Considering the benefits of frequent flyer programs, how much would you be willing to spend for membership?

1 Nothing
2 Up to $20
3 Between $20 and $30
4 Between $30 and $50
5 Between $50 and $75
6 Between $75 and $100

14e. Please rate our frequent flyer program compared to others in *(circle one for each)*

	Better	Same	Worse
program administration	3	2	1
awards	3	2	1
resolving problems	3	2	1
promotional materials	3	2	1
award redemption proce- dures	3	2	1
monthly statements	3	2	1
applications procedures	3	2	1

Section Four: Just So We Can Classify Your Answers

15. Your occupation: *(circle one)*

    1 Executive or managerial
    2 Professional
    3 Government or military
    4 Sales
    5 Student
    6 Homemaker
    7 Retired
    8 Airline/travel industry employee
    9 Other _____
    (please specify)

16. Are you self-employed? *(circle one)*   1 yes   2 no

17. Your education: *(circle one)*

    1 Some high school
    2 High school graduate
    3 Some college
    4 College graduate
    5 College post-graduate

18. Your total family annual income:

    1 Under $10,000
    2 $10,000–$19,999
    3 $20,000–$29,999
    4 $30,000–$39,999
    5 $40,000–$49,999
    6 $50,000–$59,999
    7 $60,000–$74,999
    8 $75,000–$99,999
    9 $100,000 or more

19. Your age: *(circle one)*

1 Under 18 years	4 35–49 years
2 18–24 years	5 50–64 years
3 25–34 years	6 65 or over

20. Your sex: *(circle one)*   1 male   2 female

21. Which of the following publications do you read regularly?
    (circle all that apply)

1 Your local newspaper	9 Sports Illustrated
2 Wall Street Journal	10 Savvy
3 USA Today	11 Inc.
4 New York Times	12 Forbes
5 Time	13 Working Woman
6 Newsweek	14 Business Week
7 US News & World Report	15 Money
8 People	16 Frequent Flyer Magazine

Thank you very much for your time and cooperation! Please use the space below for any additional opinions or comments that you would like us to know about.

☐ **Guest Survey**

1. How would you rate our hotel on an overall basis? ☐ Excellent ☐ Good ☐ Average ☐ Poor
2. Was your room reservation in order at check-in? ☐ Yes ☐ No
3. How would you rate the following?

	Excellent	Good	Average	Fair	Poor
Check-in speed efficiency	☐	☐	☐	☐	☐
Cleanliness of room on first entering	☐	☐	☐	☐	☐
Cleanliness and servicing of your room during stay	☐	☐	☐	☐	☐
Decor of your room	☐	☐	☐	☐	☐
Check-out speed efficiency	☐	☐	☐	☐	☐
Value of room for price paid	☐	☐	☐	☐	☐

4. Was everything in working order in your room?
☐ Yes ☐ No
If you checked NO, would you please tell us what was not in working order?
☐ Room air conditioning ☐ Television
☐ Room heating ☐ Light bulbs
☐ Bathroom plumbing ☐ Other ____

5. How would you rate the following in terms of their friendly and efficient services?

	Excellent	Good	Average	Fair	Poor
Reservation Staff	☐	☐	☐	☐	☐
Front desk clerk	☐	☐	☐	☐	☐
Bell staff	☐	☐	☐	☐	☐
Housekeeping staff	☐	☐	☐	☐	☐
Telephone operators	☐	☐	☐	☐	☐
Gift shop staff	☐	☐	☐	☐	☐
Engineering staff	☐	☐	☐	☐	☐
Front desk cashier	☐	☐	☐	☐	☐

If any members of our staff were especially helpful, please let us know who they are and how they were helpful so that we can show them our appreciation.

Name _____

Position/Comments _____

_____

6. Please rate the following which you have used on this visit.

A. *Restaurant*

Please indicate name of restaurant

_____

☐ Breakfast   ☐ Lunch   ☐ Dinner

Were you seated promptly? ☐ Yes ☐ No
Was your order taken promptly?
Was your food served promptly?

	Excellent	Good	Average	Fair	Poor
Friendly service	☐	☐	☐	☐	☐
Quality of food	☐	☐	☐	☐	☐
Menu variety	☐	☐	☐	☐	☐
Value for price paid	☐	☐	☐	☐	☐

B. Room Service

	Excellent	Good	Average	Fair	Poor
Prompt service	☐	☐	☐	☐	☐
Friendly service	☐	☐	☐	☐	☐
Quality of food	☐	☐	☐	☐	☐
Menu variety	☐	☐	☐	☐	☐
Value for price paid	☐	☐	☐	☐	☐

C. Cocktail Lounge

	Excellent	Good	Average	Fair	Poor
Prompt service	☐	☐	☐	☐	☐
Friendly service	☐	☐	☐	☐	☐
Quality of drinks	☐	☐	☐	☐	☐
Value for price paid	☐	☐	☐	☐	☐

D. Banquet/Convention Event

	Excellent	Good	Average	Fair	Poor
Prompt service	☐	☐	☐	☐	☐
Friendly service	☐	☐	☐	☐	☐
Quality of food	☐	☐	☐	☐	☐

7. Did you use "The Hot Line" to register any dissatisfaction with our hotel?

☐ No

☐ Yes, problem was resolved

☐ Yes, but problem was not resolved

Please explain any problem which remains unresolved

_____

_____

_____

8. What was the primary purpose of your visit?

☐ Pleasure ☐ Convention/group meeting banquet ☐ Business (other than above)

9. Have you stayed at this hotel previously? ☐ Yes ☐ No

10. If in the area again, would you return to this hotel? ☐ Yes ☐ No

Please print the following information:

Departure date _____

Length of stay _____

Length of stay _____ days. Room number _____

☐ Mr. ☐ Mrs. ☐ Miss ☐ Ms.

Name _____

Home address _____

_____ Zip _____

Company or organization _____

_____

Business address _____

_____ Zip _____

Thank you very much for your response. Your evaluation will make a difference.

A SAMPLE OF AN INTERNAL CLIENT SURVEY

1. Please indicate by circling your choice the degree to which the following departments/subsidiaries are responsible for your business needs:

To a very great extent	To a reasonably satisfactory extent	To a less than satisfactory extent	To a limited extent	Not applicable
1	2	3	4	5
a._____	_____	_____	_____	_____
b._____	_____	_____	_____	_____
c._____	_____	_____	_____	_____
d._____	_____	_____	_____	_____

Comments:

2. To what extent does the quality of each department/subsidiary of services meet your requirements?

To a very great extent	To a reasonably satisfactory extent	To a less than satisfactory extent	To a limited extent	Not applicable
1	2	3	4	5
a._____	_____	_____	_____	_____
b._____	_____	_____	_____	_____

c._____ _____ _____ _____ _____
d._____ _____ _____ _____ _____
Comments:

3. To what extent does each department/subsidiary jointly predetermine standards for the quality of services/products they
provide to you?

To a very great extent	To a reasonably satisfactory extent	To a less than satisfactory extent	To a limited extent	Not applicable
1	2	3	4	5
a._____	_____	_____	_____	_____
b._____	_____	_____	_____	_____
c._____	_____	_____	_____	_____
d._____	_____	_____	_____	_____

Comments:

4. To what extent are service commitments delivered to you in
a timely manner?

To a very great extent	To a reasonably satisfactory extent	To a less than satisfactory extent	To a limited extent	Not applicable
1	2	3	4	5
a._____	_____	_____	_____	_____
b._____	_____	_____	_____	_____
c._____	_____	_____	_____	_____
d._____	_____	_____	_____	_____

Comments:

5. When you have a problem outside of your department/sub-
sidiary, you know who to go to for a solution.

Definitely agree	Inclined to agree	Inclined to disagree	Definitely disagree	Undecided; don't know
1	2	3	4	5
a._____	_____	_____	_____	_____
b._____	_____	_____	_____	_____

c._____   _____   _____   _____   _____
d._____   _____   _____   _____   _____

Comments, if any:

6. To what extent do you understand the workers of the departments/subsidiaries, e.g., how they affect you and your work and how you affect their work?

	To a very great extent	To a reasonably satis- factory extent	To a less than satis- factory extent	To an extremely limited extent	Not applica- ble
a._____	1	2	3	4	5
b._____	1	2	3	4	5
c._____	1	2	3	4	5
d._____	1	2	3	4	5

Comments, if any:

7. To what extent do you feel other departments/subsidiaries understand you, your problems, difficulties, and obstacles?

	To a very great extent	To a reasonably satis- factory extent	To a less than satis- factory extent	To an extremely limited extent	Not applica- ble
a._____	1	2	3	4	5
b._____	1	2	3	4	5
c._____	1	2	3	4	5
d._____	1	2	3	4	5

Comments, if any:

8. To what extent do you feel other departments are concerned with helping you solve your problems?

	To a very great extent	To a reasonably satisfac- tory ex- tent	To a less than satis- factory extent	To an extremely limited extent	Not applica- ble
a._____	1	2	3	4	5
b._____	1	2	3	4	5
c._____	1	2	3	4	5
d._____	1	2	3	4	5

Comments, if any:

MANAGEMENT CLIMATE AND LEADERSHIP EFFECTIVENESS SURVEY RESULTS

Question	Production/Operation Management % Favor. 1-2	% Unfavor. 4-5	Marketing, Wholesale Sales Distribution % Favor. 1-2	% Unfavor. 4-5	Office, Legal, Personnel, Controller % Favor. 1-2	% Unfavor. 4-5	Overall — All three groups % Favor. 1-2	% Unfavor. 4-5
1. Members of my work unit receive regular feedback about their performance in relation to goals.	22%	77%	60%	40%	62%	37%	45%	55%
2. There is more independent effort than teamwork in my work unit	44%	55%	40%	60%	37%	62%	40%	60%
3. Members of my work unit are encouraged to think for themselves and suggest ways to improve the work environment	55%	44%	60%	40%	87%	13%	68%	32%
4. Major decisions affecting our work unit require group consensus before they are adopted	33%	66%	80%	20%	50%	50%	48%	52%
5. Management often makes decisions without explaining their rationale	87%	13%	80%	20%	87%	13%	86%	14%
6. Members of my work unit are committed to achieving our group's goals	55%	13%	40%	60%	87%	13%	64%	26%

#	Question								
7.	When a problem needs to be solved members of my group usually work together	(77%)	22%	80%	20%	74%	26%	(77%)	23%
8.	Members of my work unit are seldom asked for their opinions before decisions are made	(70%)	30%	50%	50%	37%	63%	55%	45%
9.	My coworkers and I help make the decisions about the important issues affecting us	18%	(82%)	60%	40%	50%	50%	38%	62%
10.	The rumor mill is often a better source for information than our managers	(90%)	10%	50%	50%	50%	50%	(66%)	24%
11.	Members of my work unit meet regularly to review how we are doing on our goals	40%	(60%)	40%	60%	75%	25%	(52%)	48%
12.	There is little sense of groupness in my work unit	44%	55%	40%	(60%)	25%	75%	36%	(64%)
13.	Management appreciates and uses our suggestions for improving the work unit.	44%	55%	40%	60%	62%	37%	48%	52%
14.	The and power for decision making clearly rests with management in this organization	(100%)		60%	40%	75%	25%	(83%)	17%
15.	I feel free to go to management to find out about decisions that are being made	40%	(60%)	80%	20%	87%	13%	(65%)	35%

SOME GENERAL SUGGESTIONS FOR MANAGEMENT SKILLS

❏ How to Run a Good Meeting

- Carefully prepare the agenda.
- Thoroughly know your audience.
- Thoroughly study your subject matter.
- Allow plenty of time for advance notification.
- Arrange for physical comforts.
- Follow the five steps for making a successful presentation.
- Involve the participants.
- Manage conflict.
- Obtain consensus.
- Be punctual.
- Close with a call for action.

❑ Making an Effective Presentation

Five Steps to a Successful Presentation

1. Determine your objective.
2. Plan your stategy.
3. Organize your ideas.
4. Evaluate the impact on the audience.
5. Practice.

❑ Planning Employee Performance Reviews

Goal: To make sure that each employee knows exactly what is expected of him or her and feels that this explanation is fair and reasonable.

Matters That Need to Be Communicated	*Work to Be Done by Supervisors*
Work required	Make sure the employee understands the job
Goals, plans, and programs	Keep employees informed regarding goals, plans, and programs
Relationship/importance of the employee's job	Explain organization of unit
Day-to-day problems and emergencies that arise	Review regularly with group any problems and emergencies facing the unit
Reasons for changes	Review in advance any changes affecting the group

How well the employee is
doing
How the employee feels
about objectives, plans,
goals, etc.

Conduct performance re-
views periodically
Seek out employee attitudes

❏ Compensation Discussions

Goal: To make sure that each employee knows exactly what
he or she is receiving as compensation for his or her efforts,
and feels that these rewards are fair, considerate, and in line
with his or her desires.

Matters That Need to Be Communicated	*Work to Be Done by Supervisors*
What is realistically possible as fair reward	Practical limitations made clear
How pay is determined	Make sure employees understand how pay is set
Employee benefit plans	See to it employees understand and appreciate employee benefit plans
Management's efforts to provide good working conditions	Conduct individual and group discussions regarding working conditions
Management's efforts to provide good bosses	Explain how you are a good boss
Management's efforts to provide steady work	Keep employees informed of steps to provide steady employment

Opportunities for self-development and promotion	Discuss with employees opportunities and prospects ahead
Efforts to treat employees with respect	Demonstrate through word and deed treating employees with respect
How well the employees think management is doing	Seek employees' opinions

❏ Management Skills Workshop

Workshop Objectives

1. Take advantage of the identified opportunities in the survey to improve management climate and leadership effectiveness.
2. Provide management skills training to address the issues and concerns highlighted in this survey effectively.
3. Develop participants to improve their own and their people's job performance through a participative management style.
4. Outline a "game plan" to ensure each participant's commitment to implement the programs and ideas generated through the workshop.

Day 1

Introduction

- Why we are here
- What we expect to get from this workshop.

- The need for honest, open, frank participation and involvement.

What we learned from the surveys

- Highlights of workshop leader's prior visit.
- Climate survey summary.
- Write-in comments.

Prioritization of improvement opportunities

- Group exercise.
- Four groups of five each (homogeneous).
- Select the three most important priorities and tell why.
- Who should do what, when and how?
- Chairperson reports group's finding to general assembly for overall discussion.

Which skills are most important to take advantage of the identified opportunities?

Same groups reconvene and select the six most important skills from the list attached.

- Tell why you make each selection.
- Chairperson's report to the general assembly.

What is a good boss?

- What do employees and supervisors want from their jobs and what happens if we don't provide it?
- Management style and its impact on individual behavior.

Communication skills

- Why improve your communication skills?
- Listening skills.

- Presentation skills.
- A manager's communication log.
- What needs to be communicated.
- Key ingredients for a successful meeting.

A simulated staff meeting with your supervisors/employees

Four groups of five each (mixed).
- Using the idea for successful meetings, plan and conduct the problem-solving staff meeting.
- Identify the problem you wish to solve.
- Summarize your problem, your thoughts, your solutions on the easel pad for presentation to the general assembly.

You may wish to select one item for your theme from the "write-in" comments on productivity improvement.

Day 2

Summary of previous day's learning

- How yesterday's priorities will help us to achieve our mission. (Mission statement: What kind of company do we want to be?)
- What we plan to accomplish today, i.e., pull it all together into a practical, meaningful game plan.

On productivity

- What affects it?
- Is it controllable?
- What does it cost?
- Can we manage it better?

A performance management system

- A clear statement of mission, i.e., our thrust and direction; the kind of company we want to be.

- Three to five specific shared objectives (criteria for good objectives) for each function, each unit, and each individual.
- Job descriptions for each position.
- Performance standards for each job responsibility.
- Performance appraisal and feedback.
- Training and development to improve performance.
- Individual performance planning.
- Appropriate reward system.
- Communications.

Some possible key objectives

Four groups of five each (mixed).
- Identify, in your opinion, the three most important, prioritized objectives (key results) for the organization for the period 1991–1992.
- Tell why each is important.
- What must the organization do (basic steps, actions to be taken) to achieve the objectives? Who should take this action, when and how?
- Chairperson for each group reports findings to general assembly.

The importance of job descriptions and performance standards

- What should be in a job description?
- What are performance standards and why are they important?
- One-on-one situations help to motivate people.

Six groups of three each (homogeneous).
- Select one of the job descriptions.
- Pick out the three most important specific responsibilities.
- Explain to the person responsible for doing the work the following:

- Your expectations.
- Bases/criteria on which the person's performance will be judged.
- What it will take to get a performance rating of outstanding or satisfactory or unsatisfactory.
- What kind of job he or she is doing.

Individual performance planning and performance appraisal and feedback

- A variety of individual situations.
- On delegation.
- On performance coaching.
- How to conduct a performance appraisal and review session.

Where do we go from here?

Four groups of five each (mixed).
- Identify a prioritized game plan, i.e., what you will do with the information you have learned. For example, we want your specific commitments, including timing.
- Some of the examples that you wish to consider in formulating a game plan for your group which will be translated into individual work plans are as follows:
  - Job descriptions for all managers, supervisors, and exempt staff.
  - Define clearly responsibility, accountability, authority, and working relationships.
  - Review the job and obtain agreement, each manager with his or her supervisor and each supervisor with his or her direct reports.
  - Establish performance standards for each job responsibility in conjunction and conversation with the job incumbent.
  - Review, discuss, listen, negotiate, and reach agreement.

- How management and supervisors *will* communicate more effectively.
  - Individually; one-on-one.
  - Collectively through weekly staff meetings.
  - How you *will* work more effectively together to share responsibility and accountability for the final objectives to be decided by top management based on our discussions.

- How you will delegate more effectively, i.e.,
  - Goal setting with individuals.
  - Changes in your management style, i.e., supportive, reassuring, positive, recognition, encouraging, cooperation, teamwork, and mutual support.

- Preparation and distribution of budget standards, financial targets, and expenses for each unit and each supervisor.

For each part of your plan:
- List specific steps you will take.
- When and by whom? Including beginning and ending dates.

Remember: your supervisors will receive a summary of these past two days' events. They will know what to expect. Don't disappoint them. They will also receive two days' outside training but at a more basic level in a subsequent workshop.

Workshop summary and evaluation by participants.

REFERENCES

Albrecht, K., and Zemke, R. *Service America.* Homewood, Ill.: Dow Jones-Irwin, 1985.

Ash, M. K. "On Setting Objectives." *Boardroom Reports,* May 1, 1985.

"Attention to Detail." *Chicago Magazine,* June 1985.

"An Award Winning Program." *Productivity Improvement Bulletin,* Bureau of Business Practice Publication No. 509, May 10, 1985.

Bennett, M. L., and Desatnick, R. L. *Human Resource Management in the Multinational Company.* New York: Nichols, 1978.

"Boosting Productivity." *Fast Service,* May 1981.

Bowen, D. E. "Taking Care of Human Relations Equals Taking Care of the Business." *Human Resource Reporter,* Nov. 1985.

Bradford, D. L., and Cohen, A. R. *Managing for Excellence.* New York: Wiley, 1984.

Cherrington, D. "Managers Lead by Example." *Chicago Tribune,* June 14, 1984.

"Church's Reduces Turnover and Improves Productivity." *Fast Service,* June 1981.

Crosby, P. B. *Quality Is Free*. New York: McGraw-Hill, 1980.

Crosby, P. B. *Quality Without Tears*. New York: McGraw-Hill, 1981.

Davis, S., and Wasmuth, W. "Costs of Turnover." *Cornell University H.R.A. Quarterly*, May 1983.

Denison, D. R. "Bring Corporate Culture to the Bottom Line." *Organization Dynamics*, Autumn 1984.

Desatnick, R. L. "The Role of Human Resources in Customer Service." Paper presented at Midwest Regional Conference of the American Society of Training Directors, Flint, Mich., Oct. 29, 1985.

"Developing the Management Team." *Restaurants and Institutions*, Jan. 1, 1983.

Drucker, P. F. *Managing in Turbulent Times*. New York: Harper & Row, 1980.

"Employee Training, the Food Service Cure-All." *Restaurant Hospitalty*, Apr. 1982, pp. 41–44.

Fine, S. H., and Dreyfack, R. *Customers: How to Get Them, How to Serve Them, How to Keep Them*. New York: Dartnell, 1986.

Horn, J. "Courtesy Even in Hard Times." *Nation's Restaurant News*, Sept. 2, 1985.

"Hospitals Struggle to Stay in the Pink." *Business Week*, Jan. 14, 1985.

"How to Create a More Customer-Oriented Work Force." *Personnel Adminstrator*, Oct. 1984.

"How to Prepare for Bad Times in Good Times." *Boardroom Reports*, May 1, 1985.

"KFC's Career Advancement Program." *Chain Marketing and Management*, May 17, 1984.

"KFC's National Training Center." *Restaurant Hospitality*, Apr. 1981.

LeBoeuf, M. *The Greatest Management Principle in the World*. New York: Putnam, 1985.

Lees-Haley, P., and Lees-Haley, C. "Attitude Survey Norms: A Dangerous Ally." *Personnel Administrator,* Oct. 1982, pp. 51–53.

"Marketing Drives U.S. Firms." *Food and Beverage,* June 1985.

Mescon, J. "Building on Basics." *Sky Magazine,* June 1985, pp. 34–35.

Naisbitt, J. *Megatrends.* New York: Warner, 1982.

National Restaurant Association, Human Resources Committee. *The First Day.* Chicago: National Restaurant Association, 1981.

Nevins, E. *Real Bosses Don't Say Thank You.* Somerville, N.J.: Pollyanna Press, 1983.

"New Employee Orientation." *National Restaurant Association News,* Nov. 1981.

Odiorne, G. "Avoid the Mistakes of Omission." *George Odiorne Newsletter,* Feb. 22, 1985.

O'Toole, J. *Vanguard Management.* New York: Doubleday, 1985.

Peters, T. J. "Blame the Man in the Mirror." *Success,* July/Aug. 1985.

Peters, T. J., and Austin, N. *A Passion for Excellence.* New York: Random House, 1985.

Peters, T. J., and Waterman, R. H., Jr. *In Search of Excellence.* New York: Harper & Row, 1982.

"The Power of Positive Reinforcement." *Productivity Improvement Bulletin.* Bureau of Business Practice Publication No. 515, Aug. 10, 1985.

"Product Ownership." *Productivity Improvement Bulletin,* May 1985.

"QSC Award Winners." *Insight,* Dec. 1984.

Research Institute of America. "Technical Assistance Research Program." *Money Advisory Newsletter,* June 1985.

Richman, L. S. "Tomorrow's Jobs Plentiful, But . . ." *Fortune,* Apr. 11, 1988.

St. John, W. D. "The Complete Orientation Program." *Personnel Journal,* May 1980.

Selman, C. "Design and Implementation of a Customer Service Program." Paper presented at annual meeting of American Society of Training Directors, Anaheim, Calif., May 1985.

Smith, A. *An Inquiry into the Nature and Causes of the Wealth of Nations.* (Originally published 1776.)

"Szechwan Pavilion Restaurant Review." *Chicago,* Nov. 1985.

Taylor, F. *Principles of Scientific Management.* (Originally published 1911.)

Tichy, N. M. *Managing Strategic Change.* New York: Wiley, 1983.

"Training at Pizza Hut." *Restaurant Hospitality,* Apr. 1982.

"The Transit Authority Still Struggles with Problems Faced in 1981." *New York Times,* May 23, 1985.

"The Underutilized Asset That Will Be This Decade's Single Greatest Source of Profit Growth." *Research Institute Supplement,* June 14, 1985.

"Value of Participation: A Study of the Diamond Fiber Company." *Productivity Improvement Bulletin,* May 1985.

"What Changes Would Bring about the Largest Improvements in Performance and Productivity in Most Companies?" Gallup Organization and U.S. Chamber of Commerce, June 1985.

"What Price Training?" *Restaurants and Institutions,* May 1983.

INDEX

ABOUT THE AUTHOR

Robert L. Desatnick is president and founder of Creative Human Resource Consultants, headquartered in Chicago, Illinois. Under the auspices of the firm's executive committee, he has worked with more than five hundred chief executive officers on building and maintaining customer-oriented work forces. These ongoing relationships have served as a valuable proving ground for the practical ideas, concepts, and methods in this book.

Desatnick has worked for more than twenty-five years at home and abroad in all fields of human resource management and business planning. During his career he has worked with McDonald's Corporation, as corporate vice president of human resources and worldwide senior human resource officer; Chase Manhattan Bank, as vice president and group executive for human resources; Indian Head, Inc., as corporate director for business planning and executive development; Booz, Allen & Hamilton, as consultant for professional personnel services; and General Electric Co., as MBO coordinator, management development director, seminar leader, and plant and division human resource manager.

Desatnick frequently participates in national and regional conferences of the American Society of Training Directors, the American Society for Personnel Administration, the Human Resource Planning Society, and the Foundation of the American College of Healthcare Executives. Also, for two years in succession he was one of the few business leaders selected to participate as a presenter and panelist on customer service at the world's symposiums on business achievement in Niort, France.

Desatnick is the author of numerous articles and several books on human resource management, including *A Concise Guide to Management Development, Innovative Human Resource Management, Human Resource Management in the Multinational Company, The Expanding Role of the Human Resource Manager,* and *The Business of Human Resource Management.* He received his B.S. degree with honors in liberal arts and political science from Franklin College and his M.B.A. with distinction from Washington University, where he was a Weinheimer Fellow. As a lecturer, seminar leader, and teacher, he is affiliated with several universities, including Cornell University, the University of Chicago, the University of California at Berkeley, the University of Minnesota, and DePaul University. Desatnick is also a visiting scholar at Columbia University.